STUDEBAKER HAWKS & LARKS
1956-1963

Compiled by
R.M. Clarke

ISBN 0 946489 19 X

BROOKLANDS BOOKS LTD.
P.O. BOX 146, COBHAM,
SURREY, KT11 1LG. UK

Printed in Hong Kong

BROOKLANDS BOOKS

BROOKLANDS ROAD TEST SERIES

Abarth Gold Portfolio 1950-1971
AC Ace & Aceca 1953-1983
Alfa Romeo Giulietta Gold Portfolio 1954-1965
Alfa Romeo Giulia Berlinas 1962-1976
Alfa Romeo Giulia Coupés 1963-1976
Alfa Romeo Giulia Coupés Gold P. 1963-1976
Alfa Romeo Spider 1966-1990
Alfa Romeo Spider Gold Portfolio 1966-1991
Alfa Romeo Alfasud 1972-1984
Alfa Romeo Alfetta Gold Portfolio 1972-1987
Alfa Romeo Alfetta GTV6 1980-1986
Allard Gold Portfolio 1937-1959
Alvis Gold Portfolio 1919-1967
AMX & Javelin Muscle Portfolio1968-1974
Armstrong Siddeley Gold Portfolio 1945-1960
Audi Quattro Gold Portfolio1980-1991
Austin A30 & A35 1951-1962
Austin Healey 100 & 100/6 Gold P. 1952-1959
Austin Healey 3000 Gold Portfolio 1959-1967
Austin Healey Sprite 1958-1971
Barracuda Muscle Portfolio 1964-1974
BMW Six Cyl. Coupés 1969-1975
BMW 1600 Collection No.1 1966-1981
BMW 2002 Gold Portfolio1968-1976
BMW 316, 318, 320 (4 cyl.) Gold P. 1975-1990
BMW 320, 323, 325 (6 cyl.) Gold P. 1977-1990
BMW M Series Performance Portfolio1976-1993
BMW 5 Series Gold Portfolio1981-1987
Bristol Cars Gold Portfolio 1946-1992
Buick Automobiles 1947-1960
Buick Muscle Cars 1965-1970
Cadillac Automobiles 1949-1959
Cadillac Automobiles 1960-1969
Charger Muscle Portfolio1966-1974
Chevrolet 1955-1957
Chevrolet Impala & SS 1958-1971
Chevrolet Corvair 1959-1969
Chevy II & Nova SS Muscle Portfolio 1962-1974
Chevy El Camino & SS 1959-1987
Chevelle & SS Muscle Portfolio 1964-1972
Chevrolet Muscle Cars 1966-1971
Chevy Blazer 1969-1981
Chevrolet Corvette Gold Portfolio 1953-1962
Chevrolet Corvette Sting Ray Gold P. 1963-1967
Chevrolet Corvette Gold Portfolio 1968-1977
High Performance Corvettes 1983-1989
Camaro Muscle Portfolio 1967-1973
Chevrolet Camaro Z28 & SS 1966-1973
Chevrolet Camaro & Z28 1973-1981
High Performance Camaros 1982-1988
Chrysler 300 Gold Portfolio 1955-1970
Chrysler Valiant 1960-1962
Citroen Traction Avant Gold Portfolio 1934-1957
Citroen 2CV Gold Portfolio 1948-1989
Citroen DS & ID 1955-1975
Citroen DS & ID Gold Portfolio 1955-1975
Citroen SM 1970-1975
Cobras & Replicas 1962-1983
Shelby Cobra Gold Portfolio 1962-1969
Cobras & Cobra Replicas Gold P. 1962-1989
Cunningham Automobiles 1951-1955
Daimler SP250 Sports & V-8 250 Saloon Gold Portfolio 1959-1969
Datsun Roadsters 1962-1971
Datsun 240Z 1970-1973
Datsun 280Z & ZX 1975-1983
The De Lorean 1977-1993
Dodge Muscle Cars 1967-1970
Dodge Viper on the Road
ERA Gold Portfolio 1934-1994
Excalibur Collection No. 1 1952-1981
Facel Vega 1954-1964
Ferrari Dino 1965-1974
Ferrari Dino 308 1974-1979
Ferrari 308 & Mondial 1980-1984
Fiat 500 Gold Portfolio 1936-1972
Fiat 600 & 850 Gold Portfolio 1955-1972
Fiat Pininfarina 124 & 2000 Spider 1968-1985
Fiat-Bertone X1/9 1973-1988
Ford Consul, Zephyr, Zodiac Mk.I & II 1950-1962
Ford Zephyr, Zodiac, Executive, Mk.III & Mk.IV 1962-1971
Ford Cortina 1600E & GT 1967-1970
High Performance Capris Gold P. 1969-1987
Capri Muscle Portfolio 1974-1987
High Performance Fiestas 1979-1991
High Performance Escorts Mk.I 1968-1974
High Performance Escorts Mk.II 1975-1980
High Performance Escorts 1980-1985
High Performance Escorts 1985-1990
High Performance Sierras & Merkurs Gold POrtfolio 1983-1990
Ford Automobiles 1949-1959
Ford Fairlane 1955-1970
Ford Ranchero 1957-1959
Ford Thunderbird 1955-1957
Ford Thunderbird 1958-1963
Ford Thunderbird 1964-1976
Ford GT40 Gold Portfolio 1964-1987
Ford Bronco 1966-1977
Ford Bronco 1978-1988
Holden 1948-1962
Honda CRX 1983-1987
International Scout Gold Portfolio 1961-1980
Isetta 1953-1964
ISO & Bizzarrini Gold Portfolio 1962-1974
Jaguar and SS Gold Portfolio 1931-1951
Jaguar XK120, 140, 150 Gold P. 1948-1960
Jaguar Mk.VII, VIII, IX, X, 420 Gold P.1950-1970
Jaguar Mk.1 & Mk.2 Gold Portfolio 1959-1969
Jaguar E-Type Gold Portfolio 1961-1971
Jaguar E-Type V-12 1971-1975
Jaguar XJ12, XJ5.3, V12 Gold P. 1972-1990
Jaguar XJ6 Series I & II Gold P. 1968-1979
Jaguar XJ6 Series III 1979-1986
Jaguar XJS Gold Portfolio 1975-1988
Jeep CJ5 & CJ6 1960-1976
Jeep CJ5 & CJ7 1976-1986
Jensen Cars 1946-1967
Jensen Cars 1967-1979
Jensen Interceptor Gold Portfolio 1966-1986
Jensen Healey 1972-1976
Lagonda Gold Portfolio 1919-1964
Lamborghini Countach & Urraco 1974-1980
Lamborghini Countach & Jalpa 1980-1985
Lancia Fulvia Gold Portfolio 1963-1976
Lancia Beta Gold Portfolio 1972-1984
Lancia Delta Gold Portfolio 1979-1994
Lancia Stratos 1972-1985
Land Rover Series I 1948-1958
Land Rover Series II & IIa 1958-1971
Land Rover Series III 1971-1985
Land Rover 90 & 110 Defender Gold Portfolio 1983-1994
Land Rover Discovery 1989-1994
Lincoln Gold Portfolio 1949-1960
Lincoln Continental 1961-1969
Lincoln Continental 1969-1976
Lotus Sports Racers Gold Portfolio 1953-1965
Lotus & Caterham Seven Gold P. 1957-1989
Lotus Elite 1957-1964
Lotus Elite & Eclat 1974-1982
Lotus Elan Gold Portfolio 1962-1974
Lotus Elan Collection No. 2 1963-1972
Lotus Elan & SE 1989-1992
Lotus Cortina Gold Portfolio 1963-1970
Lotus Europa Gold Portfolio 1966-1975
Lotus Elite & Eclat 1974-1982
Lotus Turbo Esprit 1980-1986
Marcos Cars 1960-1988
Maserati 1965-1970
Maserati 1970-1975
Mercedes 190 & 300 SL 1954-1963
Mercedes 230/250/280SL 1963-1971
Mercedes Benz SLs & SLCs Gold P. 1971-1989
Mercedes S & 600 1965-1972
Mercedes S Class 1972-1979
Mercedes SLs Performance Portfolio 1989-1994
Mercury Muscle Cars 1966-1971
Messerschmitt Gold Portfolio1954-1964
MG Gold Portfolio 1929-1939
MG TC 1945-1949
MG TD 1949-1953
MG TF 1953-1955
MGA & Twin Cam Gold Portfolio 1955-1962
MG Midget Gold Portfolio1961-1979
MGB Roadsters 1962-1980
MGB MGC & V8 Gold Portfolio 1962-1980
MGB GT 1965-1980
Mini Gold Portfolio 1959-1969
Mini Gold Portfolio 1969-1980
Mini Cooper Gold Portfolio 1961-1971
Mini Muscle Cars 1961-1979
Mini Moke Gold Portfolio1964-1994
Mopar Muscle Cars 1964-1967
Morgan Three-Wheeler Gold Portfolio 1910-1952
Morgan Plus 4 & Four 4 Gold P. 1936-1967
Morgan Cars 1960-1970
Morgan Cars Gold Portfolio 1968-1989
Morris Minor Collection No. 1 1948-1980
Shelby Mustang Muscle Portfolio 1965-1970
High Performance Mustang IIs 1974-1978
High Performance Mustangs 1982-1988
Nash-Austin Metropolitan Gold P.1954-1962
Oldsmobile Automobiles 1955-1963
Oldsmobile Muscle Cars 1964-1971
Oldsmobile Toronado 1966-1978
Opel GT 1968-1973
Packard Gold Portfolio 1946-1958
Pantera Gold Portfolio 1970-1989
Panther Gold Portfolio 1972-1990
Plymouth Muscle Cars 1966-1971
Pontiac Tempest & GTO 1961-1965
Pontiac Muscle Cars 1966-1972
Pontiac Firebird & Trans-Am 1973-1981
High Performance Firebirds 1982-1988
Pontiac Fiero 1984-1988
Porsche 356 Gold Portfolio1953-1965
Porsche 911 1965-1969
Porsche 911 1970-1972
Porsche 911 1973-1977
Porsche 911 Carrera 1973-1977
Porsche 911 Turbo 1975-1984
Porsche 911 SC 1978-1983
Porsche 914 Collection No. 1 1969-1983
Porsche 914 Gold Portfolio 1969-1976
Porsche 924 Gold Portfolio 1975-1988
Porsche 928 Performance Portfolio 1977-1994
Porsche 944 Gold Portfolio1981-1991
Range Rover Gold Portfolio 1970-1992
Reliant Scimitar 1964-1986
Riley Gold Portfolio 1924-1939
Riley 1.5 & 2.5 Litre Gold Portfolio 1945-1955
Rolls Royce Silver Cloud & Bentley 'S' Series Gold Portfolio 1955-1965
Rolls Royce Silver Shadow Gold P. 1965-1980
Rolls Royce & Bentley Gold P. 1980-1989
Rover P4 1949-1959
Rover P4 1955-1964
Rover 3 & 3.5 Litre Gold Portfolio 1958-1973
Rover 2000 & 2200 1963-1977
Rover 3500 1968-1977
Rover 3500 & Vitesse 1976-1986
Saab Sonett Collection No.1 1966-1974
Saab Turbo 1976-1983
Studebaker Gold Portfolio 1947-1966
Studebaker Hawks & Larks 1956-1963
Avanti 1962-1990
Sunbeam Tiger & Alpine Gold P. 1959-1967
Toyota MR2 1984-1988
Toyota Land Cruiser 1956-1984
Triumph TR2 & TR3 Gold Portfolio 1952-1961
Triumph TR4, TR5, TR250 1961-1968
Triumph TR6 Gold Portfolio 1969-1976
Triumph TR7 & TR8 Gold Portfolio 1975-1982
Triumph Herald 1959-1971
Triumph Vitesse 1962-1971
Triumph Spitfire Gold Portfolio 1962-1980
Triumph 2000, 2.5, 2500 1963-1977
Triumph GT6 Gold Portfolio 1966-1974
Triumph Stag 1970-1980
TVR Gold Portfolio 1959-1986
TVR Performance Portfolio 1986-1994
VW Beetle Gold Portfolio1935-1967
VW Beetle Gold Portfolio1968-1991
VW Beetle Collection No.1 1970-1982
VW Karmann Ghia 1955-1982
VW Bus, Camper, Van 1954-1967
VW Bus, Camper, Van 1968-1979
VW Bus, Camper, Van 1979-1989
VW Scirocco 1974-1981
VW Golf GTI 1976-1986
Volvo PV444 & PV544 1945-1965
Volvo Amazon-120 Gold Portfolio 1956-1970
Volvo 1800 Gold Portfolio 1960-1973

BROOKLANDS ROAD & TRACK SERIES

Road & Track on Alfa Romeo 1949-1963
Road & Track on Alfa Romeo 1964-1970
Road & Track on Alfa Romeo 1971-1976
Road & Track on Alfa Romeo 1977-1989
Road & Track on Aston Martin 1962-1990
R & T on Auburn Cord and Duesenburg 1952-84
Road & Track on Audi & Auto Union 1952-1980
Road & Track on Audi & Auto Union 1980-1986
Road & Track on Austin Healey 1953-1970
Road & Track on BMW Cars 1966-1974
Road & Track on BMW Cars 1975-1978
Road & Track on BMW Cars 1979-1983
R & T on Cobra, Shelby & Ford GT40 1962-1992
Road & Track on Corvette 1953-1967
Road & Track on Corvette 1968-1982
Road & Track on Corvette 1982-1986
Road & Track on Corvette 1986-1990
Road & Track on Datsun Z 1970-1983
Road & Track on Ferrari 1975-1981
Road & Track on Ferrari 1981-1984
Road & Track on Ferrari 1984-1988
Road & Track on Fiat Sports Cars 1968-1987
Road & Track on Jaguar 1950-1960
Road & Track on Jaguar 1961-1968
Road & Track on Jaguar 1968-1974
Road & Track on Jaguar 1974-1982
Road & Track on Jaguar 1983-1989
Road & Track on Lamborghini 1964-1985
Road & Track on Lotus 1972-1981
Road & Track on Maserati 1952-1974
Road & Track on Maserati 1975-1983
R & T on Mazda RX7 & MX5 Miata 1986-1991
Road & Track on Mercedes 1952-1962
Road & Track on Mercedes 1963-1970
Road & Track on Mercedes 1971-1979
Road & Track on Mercedes 1980-1987
Road & Track on MG Sports Cars 1949-1961
Road & Track on MG Sports Cars 1962-1980
Road & Track on Mustang 1964-1977
R & T on Nissan 300-ZX & Turbo 1984-1989
Road & Track on Peugeot 1955-1986
Road & Track on Pontiac 1960-1983
Road & Track on Porsche 1951-1967
Road & Track on Porsche 1968-1971
Road & Track on Porsche 1972-1975
Road & Track on Porsche 1975-1978
Road & Track on Porsche 1979-1982
Road & Track on Porsche 1982-1985
Road & Track on Porsche 1985-1988
R & T on Rolls Royce & Bentley 1950-1965
R & T on Rolls Royce & Bentley 1966-1984
Road & Track on Saab 1972-1992
R & T on Toyota Sports & GT Cars 1966-1984
R & T on Triumph Sports Cars 1953-1967
R & T on Triumph Sports Cars 1967-1974
R & T on Triumph Sports Cars 1974-1982
Road & Track on Volkswagen 1951-1968
Road & Track on Volkswagen 1968-1978
Road & Track on Volkswagen 1978-1985
Road & Track on Volvo 1957-1974
Road & Track on Volvo 1977-1994
R&T - Henry Manney at Large & Abroad
R&T - Peter Egan's "Side Glances"

BROOKLANDS CAR AND DRIVER SERIES

Car and Driver on BMW 1955-1977
Car and Driver on BMW 1977-1985
C and D on Cobra, Shelby & Ford GT40 1963-84
Car and Driver on Corvette 1956-1967
Car and Driver on Corvette 1968-1977
Car and Driver on Corvette 1978-1982
Car and Driver on Corvette 1983-1988
C and D on Datsun Z 1600 & 2000 1966-1984
Car and Driver on Ferrari 1955-1962
Car and Driver on Ferrari 1963-1975
Car and Driver on Ferrari 1976-1983
Car and Driver on Mopar 1956-1967
Car and Driver on Mopar 1968-1975
Car and Driver on Mustang 1964-1972
Car and Driver on Pontiac 1961-1975
Car and Driver on Porsche 1955-1962
Car and Driver on Porsche 1963-1970
Car and Driver on Porsche 1970-1976
Car and Driver on Porsche 1977-1981
Car and Driver on Porsche 1982-1986
Car and Driver on Saab 1956-1985
Car and Driver on Volvo 1955-1986

BROOKLANDS PRACTICAL CLASSICS SERIES

PC on Austin A40 Restoration
PC on Land Rover Restoration
PC on Metalworking in Restoration
PC on Midget/Sprite Restoration
PC on Mini Cooper Restoration
PC on MGB Restoration
PC on Morris Minor Restoration
PC on Sunbeam Rapier Restoration
PC on Triumph Herald/Vitesse
PC on Spitfire Restoration
PC on Beetle Restoration
PC on 1930s Car Restoration

BROOKLANDS HOT ROD 'MUSCLECAR & HI-PO ENGINES' SERIES

Chevy 265 & 283
Chevy 302 & 327
Chevy 348 & 409
Chevy 350 & 400
Chevy 396 & 427
Chevy 454 thru 512
Chrysler Hemi
Chrysler 273, 318, 340 & 360
Chrysler 361, 383, 400, 413, 426, 440
Ford 289, 302, Boss 302 & 351W
Ford 351C & Boss 351
Ford Big Block

BROOKLANDS RESTORATION SERIES

Auto Restoration Tips & Techniques
Basic Bodywork Tips & Techniques
Basic Painting Tips & Techniques
Camaro Restoration Tips & Techniques
Chevrolet High Performance Tips & Techniques
Chevy Engine Swapping Tips & Techniques
Chevy-GMC Pickup Repair
Chrysler Engine Swapping Tips & Techniques
Custom Painting Tips & Techniques
Engine Swapping Tips & Techniques
Ford Pickup Repair
How to Build a Street Rod
Land Rover Restoration Tips & Techniques
MG 'T' Series Restoration Guide
Mustang Restoration Tips & Techniques
Performance Tuning - Chevrolets of the '60's
Performance Tuning - Pontiacs of the '60's

BROOKLANDS MILITARY VEHICLES SERIES

Allied Military Vehicles No.1 1942-1945
Allied Military Vehicles No.2 1941-1946
Complete WW2 Military Jeep Manual
Dodge Military Vehicles No.1 1940-1945
Hail To The Jeep
Land Rovers in Military Service
Mil. & Civ Amphibians 1940-1990
Off Road Jeeps: Civ. & Mil. 1944-1971
US Military Vehicles 1941-1945
US Army Military Vehicles WW2-TM9-2800
VW Kubelwagen Military Portfolio1940-1990
WW2 Jeep Military Portfolio 1941-1945
21124

BROOKLANDS
BOOKS

CONTENTS

BROOKLANDS BOOKS

ACKNOWLEDGEMENTS

Earlier today I received a letter from a gentleman in Los Angeles enquiring about a photograph of his car that appears on the cover of our AC Cobra book. It, like the majority of pictures we use in this position, was shot whilst parked unattended in some innocent location. There have been Firebirds in Florida, Land Rovers in Sydney, Porsches in Carmel, Stags in London and now a Hawk in Vancouver and I sincerely hope we have done justice to this handsome vehicle.

The excellent Car Collector article which follows puts the Hawks and Larks into perspective and eliminates the need for a formal introduction to these models.

It is twenty years ago to the month that the last Studebakers left the line at South Bend. We hope that on the one hand this book will act as a tribute to the marque and on the other encourage owners of these elegant machines to cherish and preserve them for us all to enjoy. The Brooklands reference series is produced in the main for owners and restorers. They exist because the publishers of the world's leading automotive journals understand the needs of enthusiasts and generously allow us to include their interesting copyright stories. Our thanks, combined with those of Studebaker devotees, go to the publishers of Auto Age, Autocar, Autosport, Car & Driver, Car Collector, Car Life, Modern Motor, Motor, Motor Sport Illustrated, Road & Track, Speed Age, Track & Traffic and Wheels for their continued support.

R.M. Clarke

Aviculture in South Bend:

The Story of the Studebaker Hawks

The motivating factors behind the creation of the original Studebaker Hawks in 1956 came from at least three different sources. The first and perhaps most significant was Studebaker's own history, particularly that since the end of the Second World War. In 1947, Studebaker had proclaimed itself rather immodestly and somewhat inaccurately as "first by far with a post-war car". Whereas the new-look Studebakers first appeared in the summer of 1947, automotive upstart Henry Kaiser and his partner, Joseph Frazer, had constructed 11,751 Kaisers and Frazers in 1946. Neither design can lay claim to possession of a form that qualifies for consideration as a great artistic achievement. Yet in the case of Studebaker, an interesting policy, namely the offering of a stylish coupe body design that bore a sibling resemblance to its two and four door brethren and yet had its own distinct personality, *was* noteworthy. The Starlight coupe was only 61 inches high, and with its wraparound rear

windows, was one of the most distinctive-appearing new automobiles on the American road. Like the Model T Ford it was the butt of numerous jokes, nearly all of which centered around the theme of "which way is it going?" The jokes were mostly all bad but they didn't harm the sale of Studebakers in the years from 1947 through 1950. In 1947, Studebaker built over 123,000 cars, the following year almost 165,000. After trailing Kaiser-Frazer both years, Studebaker vaulted into fourth place in production in 1949. The weakest of the Big Three, at that time the Ford Motor Company, was out of reach with a total production of 1,077,600 vehicles but Studebaker led all the independents with an output of 228,400 vehicles. Whereas the slabsided Kaisers and Frazers had quickly lost appeal with customers (only 60,400 were built in 1949), the Studebaker, in the face of all new models from GM, Ford, and Chrysler, had increased its share of the production pie from 4.21% in 1948 to

4.45% in 1949. Studebaker enjoyed another good year in 1950, with its P-51 front-end (production just exceeded 268,000), but the following year output dropped to 222,000. Within the Studebaker organization, or, more accurately, in the Raymond Loewy studios, work was well under way on an automobile that would not only replace the now somewhat-dated Starlite coupe but would be recognized as one of the most aesthetically pleasing automobiles ever built in the United States.

In 1950, General Motors received perhaps ten times the cost of developing the LeSabre show car in the form of publicity that didn't cost a penny. From *The New York Daily News* to Britain's, *The Autocar*, readers throughout the world ogled (and also found fault with) Harley Earl's creation. On a smaller scale, both physically and financially, Nash-Kelvinator reaped similar benefits with the NXI which later went into production as the Metropolitan. There was nothing unusual, therefore, in

Fender lights and two-tone paint treatment add nothing to this 1956 Studebaker Golden Hawk. A prime example of the senselessness of year-by-year model changes for the sake of change. BOB ACKERSON COLLECTION

Studebaker's decision in early 1951 to produce a show car of its own. Perhaps the only unique feature of its development was that, whereas GM styling was an integral part of the General Motors' corporate structure, Studebaker was farming out its dream car assignment to an independent styling firm, in this case the aforementioned Raymond Loewy.

Primary responsibility for the Studebaker show car's appearance was delegated to Robert Bourke. Bourke's involvement with Studebaker dated back to the last years of the war when the Loewy staff was under contract to prepare designs for a new post-war Studebaker. Although Virgil Exner is credited with designing the 1947 Studebakers, both Loewy and Bourke are also to be credited with its appearance since all three men worked together on the Studebaker assignment until Loewy and Exner went their separate ways.

Now, years later, Bourke was, along with stylist Bob Koto, engaged not only on the show car project but on a full line of proposals for production cars and trucks that Loewy hoped would find favor with Messrs. Paul G. Hoffman and Harold Vance, the head honchos at Studebaker.

Bourke's efforts from start to finish were observed with obvious interest by the Studebaker management. The leadership at Studebaker, while guilty of future misdeeds (at least in the eyes of those who revere Studebaker as a

producer of automobiles), was at this time more prone to move ahead of the crowd than let GM do their thinking for them. The risk of being too different was known to them, of course, but equally a part of their collective outlook was the awareness that to survive Studebaker had to dare to be different. In 1939, the Loewy-styled Studebaker Champion had turned the company around. The appeal of the 1947-1952 Studebakers had been proved by their sales. Thus the decision of the Studebaker directors to place the Bourke show car into production was in the perspective of Studebaker history not all that much of a surprise.

Unfortunately, in 1953, when the production version of Bourke's design appeared in the form of a Starliner hardtop coupe and a pillared five-window version known as the Starlight, the pieces were starting to come apart at Studebaker. Production delays cooled many a buyers' enthusiasm for a new Studebaker coupe and the sight of a 1953 Studebaker already bearing the bubbles of rust after barely one year of road use was not a development likely to fill the corporate coffers at South Bend.

Studebaker production for 1953 and 1954 was nothing less than nightmarish. Instead of attaining a hoped-for output in 1953 of 350,000 units, Studebaker production for 1953 and 1954 tallied just 271,800. The situation assumed far more critical proportions when 1954

is examined as a single entity. Production fell to 85,300 and Studebaker's segment of the market dropped below 2%.

The restyling of the Loewy coupes, the Starliner version of which was rated by *Fortune* magazine as the fourth-best-designed product of the Industrial Age, was a move that failed to impress styling critics. Nor did it send customers flocking to Studebaker showrooms. Yet out of the desperation of the hour and the concurrent merger of Studebaker and Packard came the blending of the elements leading to the emergence, in 1956, of the Studebaker Hawks, surely among the more desirable collector cars of the post-war years.

The immediate predecessor of the Hawk was a sporticized version of the 1955 Studebaker President coupe known as the Speedster. Studebaker debuted its 1955 lineup before the other automobile manufacturers that year in an effort to garner as much publicity as possible. Along with its new chrome look and price reductions, Studebaker also gave plenty of exposure to the Speedster, which was portrayed as a "secret dream car" and a limited production run of 20 was supposedly planned. With simulated wire wheel covers, built-in fog lights, and a chrome "earmuff" just forward of the rear window, the Speedster was showy but not necessarily offensive. In the interior, a fiberglass dash with an artificial, but good-looking, engine-turned insert surrounded a bevy of Borg-Warner white-on-black instruments, including a tach reading to 8000 rpm and a speedometer reading to 160 mph. These features, plus the Speedster's diamond stitched top grain leather upholstery and sidepanels, attracted enough attention to persuade Studebaker to introduce it as a production car early in 1955. Described by Studebaker as an automobile "designed to appeal particularly to owners who desire special sports car styling and performance with traditional American car comfort", the Speedster has long played second fiddle to the more dramatically-styled and powered Hawks that were to follow. Yet when seen as a link in the development of the American high performance automobile, the Speedster deserves some recognition.

The Speedsters were equipped with

CAR COLLECTOR

the 259.2 cid V-8 that also powered the revived President models in 1955. With a four-barrel Carter carburetor and dual exhausts, its output was 185 hp at 4500 rpm. *Motor Life* for June, 1955, found it a satisfying automobile, capable of zero to sixty runs (with automatic transmission) in the ten second range and with the exception of its rather slow steering (4½ turns lock to lock), possessing handling that was above par when compared to its contemporaries.

Studebaker's last effort to do battle head on with the Big Three came in 1956. The entire Studebaker lineup was given a thorough and expensive going over and in place of the Speedster there emerged a quartet of Studebaker Hawks.

GOLDEN HAWK

To those who admired the original Loewy design of 1953, the Hawks were no doubt an aberration. Yet if nothing else their appearance conveyed a sense of power that somehow was lacking in the earlier coupes. The Golden Hawk wasn't the most powerful American car, but at 275 hp it wasn't exactly a 97-pound weakling either. The Golden Hawk engine was identical to that used in the 1956 Packard Clipper. There was much to be admired in the design of that 352 cid V-8 but at 725 pounds, it was to forever endow the Golden Hawk with a reputation as one of the most ill-handling American automobiles of the mid-fifties. Surprisingly, however, a perusal of Golden Hawk road tests results in the discovery of a rather interesting diversity of views expressed in regard to its handling qualities. In a three-way Thunderbird-Corvette-Golden Hawk test by Jimmy Reece (*Speed Age*, July 1956), the extreme front end weight bias of the Hawk led Reece to write rather harsh words about its cornering competence. "On severe turns, there was a tremendous amount of body roll", Reece wrote, "causing the rear wheel to lift and break traction. On one severe curve, the roll-over was so extensive that it placed a tell-tale black mark almost down to the white sidewall of the tires". *Auto Age* (March, 1956) was more charitable but less accurate by noting that the "Golden Hawk does lean when cornered hard, but less than any

other five-passenger American automobile". But if handling was not the Golden Hawk's best act, its acceleration in a straight line needed no apologies. With Ultramatic transmission, zero to 60 mph runs were in the nine second range. Stick-shift Golden Hawks did even better, usually breaking the eight second mark.

SKY HAWK

Definitely not in the same class as the Golden Hawk was the Sky Hawk, which like its big brother was a pillarless hardtop coupe. Unlike the Golden Hawk, it relied on the Studebaker engine (which dated back to 1951) for its source of power. This power plant wasn't a featherweight either, but it *was* lighter that the Packard engine and with either 210 hp (two-barrel carburetor) or 225 hp (four-barrel carburetor), it was probably the Hawk with the best-balanced overall performance in 1956.

POWER and FLIGHT HAWKS

Studebaker rounded out its Hawk lineup with two five-window coupes, the Power and Flight Hawks; the first of which was powered by a 259.2 cid V-8 available either in 180 hp or 195 hp form. The Flight Hawk had to make do with the veteran L-head six that dated back to the pre-war Champion. In its 1956 guise it managed to reap a modest 101 hp from 170 cubic inches.

Many Studebaker historians tend to expound on the virtues of the lesser Hawks and criticize the Golden Hawk for its fins and overburdened front end. But somehow the feeling persists that perhaps these critics are missing an important point. Throughout their production life the Hawks were often characterized as cars that could have followed a developmental pattern not unlike that of the Corvette. The Hawk, this view maintains, could have become a true Grand Touring car if Studebaker had played its cards right. But Studebaker didn't have the means to duplicate, along GT lines, what Duntov and Mitchell did for the Corvette. They had to make do with what they had and if, in 1956, the most potent Hawk available was only rated at 225 horsepower, the company would have been nowhere in the performance race. At least with the Golden Hawk, Studebaker was in the midst of the fray. In the final analysis, it probably didn't matter very much but when Studebaker could depict the Golden Hawk as one of America's most powerful automobiles, it surely wasn't *worse* off for the effort. Thus the image of the Hawk as a high performance automobile, while never totally exploited, was at least initiated by the existence of the first Golden Hawk.

The following year, with the Packard engine out of production, Studebaker had to revert to use of the 289 cid inch V-8 to power the Golden Hawk.

This 1957 Silver Hawk coupe benefited little from the addition of the then-popular tail fins. BOB ACKERSON COLLECTION

The top-of-the-line: The 1957 Studebaker Golden Hawk boasted 275 supercharged horse-power and is identifiable by its louvered hood-bulge. BOB ACKERSON COLLECTION

Like its independent compatriot, Kaiser-Frazer, which had been caught up short in the horsepower race of the early fifties, Studebaker decided to go the supercharged route as a means of bridging the gap between itself and its competition. There was, however, one important distinction. Whereas Kaiser was trying to square off against its OHV V-8-armed competition with an obsolete flathead six, Studebaker had a modern, if heavy, and somewhat small, OHV V-8 available. Thus by using the same McCulloch supercharger as used on 1954 vintage Kaisers, Studebaker was able to claim a 275 hp rating for its 1957 Golden Hawk. This enabled it to maintain essentially the same performance level as the Packard-engined Hawk without that model's poor handling. The 1957 Golden Hawk was still not a handling masterpiece but now, at least, it was within the bounds of acceptability.

Studebaker reduced the Hawk brood to just two models for 1957, the Golden Hawk and the Silver Hawk, in effect, a combination of the Sky Hawk engine and the Power/Flight Hawk body. Both the Golden and Silver Hawk were, depending upon your viewpoint, blessed or cursed with large fiberglass fins. Through 1961, these canted fins were a Hawk characteristic and aren't as offensive today as some other examples of that baroque era in automobile styling.

Studebaker-Packard fortunes in 1957 and 1958 were hardly awe-inspiring.

Sales declined steadily. In 1957, production totalled only 72,000. The following year, 56,900. The Hawks were, given all the bad press and despite the recession of 1958, were surprisingly good sellers. From 1957 through 1958, nearly 28,000 Golden and Silver Hawks were produced. Yet the Hawk was an expensive automobile to manufacture and by its very nature would never achieve a sales volume even remotely close to Studebaker's break-even point. To achieve that end, Studebaker abandoned Nance's full-line strategy in 1959 and placed all its corporate resources behind the Lark. For a time the Lark did rather well, returning Studebaker to profitable operation in 1959. At this point the success of its younger sibling very nearly brought the Hawk to the end of its production life. Only the insistence of many Studebaker dealers that it served a useful purpose as a showroom traffic stimulator stood between the Hawk and oblivion.

The Hawk was continued for 1959 but only in Silver Hawk coupe form and minus the supercharged engine of the Golden Hawk. Instead, the most potent engine available was the veteran 259.2 cid V-8 which, with dual exhausts and four-barrel carburetor, developed 195 hp. Acceleration with Flightomatic was modest. Zero to sixty in 13.8 seconds probably brought tears to the eyes of those who had personally experienced the accelerating prowess of the earlier versions of the Hawks.

Partial restitution of the Hawk's performance potential took place in 1960, when the 289 cid V-8, either with 210 or 225 hp, was made the standard Hawk engine. Styling changes made in 1960 and 1961 to Studebaker's venerable coupe (known only as the Studebaker Hawk for those two years) were minimal, consisting only of a slight revamping of the side trim on the fins and redesigned fender and grille badges.

Studebaker emphasized the 1961 Hawk as a limited production automobile of which just 6,100 would be manufactured. The fact that Studebaker failed to reach even this modest quota (only 3,929 1961 Hawks were built) reflects more on the "old hat" image the Hawk suffered from than on the merits of the automobile itself. In

The 1960 Studebaker Hawks were changed little from previous years, as company finances did not permit massive revision. BOB ACKERSON COLLECTION

Studebaker Hawk

reality the 1961 Hawk was, since the Borg-Warner all-synchromesh four-speed transmission was available as an option, the most desirable Hawk built up to that point from the enthusiasts' point of view. Perhaps *Motor Life* (June, 1961) put the Hawk in its proper place in the automobile spectrum by noting, "The Hawk is no sports car but it is very close to an American Gran Turismo — with good handling, 120 mph top speed, adequate passenger and luggage space, and full weather protection."

If the Hawk was such a fine automobile, why were only 3,929 produced in 1961? Undoubtedly its appearance played a major factor. Its basic body shell dated back, of course, to 1953 and in its Hawk form, hadn't really undergone any substantial change since 1956. Furthermore, Studebaker's lukewarm attitude toward continuing Hawk production had led to confusion in the public's eye as to what type of car the Hawk actually was. As a high performance car, at least in the American idiom, it was a non-qualifier. True, it was a nicely-balanced package of performance, handling, and braking, but with only 225 hp it was no match for the likes of the Chevrolet 409s, Chrysler 413s and the 405 hp Fords. Nor was the Hawk embraced by the sports car fraternity as a Greek brother. Its long, 120.5" wheelbase and heavy engine were simply not the features likely to attract Austin-Healey Sprite or MG owners looking to move up on the sports car totem pole. *Road & Track* was generous with its praise of the Studebaker Hawk and found much worthy of note. However, it concluded its commentary by cautioning Hawk drivers against attempting to follow an Alfa Romeo into a decreasing radius turn. Enough said about the Hawk's sports car handling.

Some magazines, such as *Motor Trend* (July, 1959), depicted the Hawk as a "simple, functional automobile" Nothing was wrong with being such a vehicle, of course, but few people looking for a utilitarian vehicle were likely to even consider the $3,100 Hawk. A Rambler American was much more of a logical choice.

The most promising avenue for the promotion of the Hawk seemed to be as

The Hawk hand-made metal prototype, built by Brooks Stevens Associates. Clay models were established from this driveable, full-size model, an unusual practice. BROOKS STEVENS PHOTO

Comparison of this and previous photo shows that few changes were made from Stevens' prototype to this final 1962 Gran Turismo Hawk. BOB ACKERSON COLLECTION

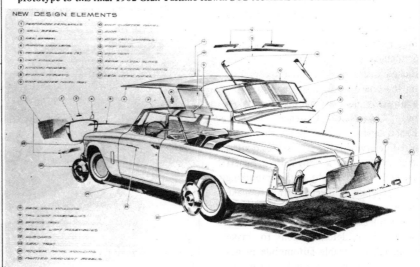

This photo shows the various components Stevens devised or modified to create the GT Hawk from the earlier car. BROOKS STEVENS PHOTO

Brook Stevens' Hawk Sceptre prototype. Headlight arrangement uses an experimental Sylvania tube-type bulb. Photo courtesy Brooks Stevens.

an elegant, prestige car with overtones of sportinesss and high performance.

At this point, in 1961, Studebaker had experienced another episode in the continuing power struggle between the elements inside the corporation who wanted Studebaker to abandon automobile production and those who were committed to Studebaker's continued presence in the automobile industry. The pro-car forces were led by Harold Churchill who had at least temporarily stemmed the flow of red ink across Studebaker's ledgers with the Lark. Regardless of how that "new dimension in motoring" was viewed, it was a stop-gap effort at best. Churchill knew that and so did just about everyone else in the industry. He wanted Studebaker to follow up the Lark's minor triumph in 1959 with all-new Studebakers in 1960. On this point he locked horns with the anti-automobilists on the board of directors, and lost. For a time his place as chairman was taken by 72-year-old Clarence Francis. Exactly why at this point the board hired Sherwood Egbert as President is somewhat of a mystery. Egbert certainly did the right thing, embarking on a program of diversification to make happy both the Studebaker board and the Studebaker creditors. Yet he also possessed a determination to make Studebaker a viable automobile manufacturer. Whether or not Egbert would have succeeded if his health hadn't failed him, poses much food for

thought. He had many obstacles to overcome but he also had a great deal going for him. Not the least of these was his iconoclastic attitude toward the sacred cows of the automobile industry. He knew what had to be done and was not bound by convention when it came to seeking solutions. But any path of reconstruction had to be lightly trod. Because Studebaker didn't have much money to play with, for a time Egbert had to spruce up the rather tarnished and bedraggled Studebaker image with automobiles whose design was well over a decade old.

This was, of course, the plight of all the independents at one point or

another in the post-war years. Perhaps the champion problem solver in this regard was Brooks Stevens, who had designed the original Jeepster on a financial shoe-string. His numerous other designs, such as the Willys FC150-170 trucks, were characterized by their low tooling costs. In 1960, Stevens had facelifted the old Willys Aero sedan for production in Brazil. Yet the result was extremely effective and seemed to Egbert to suggest a lesson from which Studebaker could profit. Specifically, Egbert reasoned if Stevens could do wonders with an obsolete Willys body shell, he could certainly be extremely effective with a design that in its original form had been a masterpiece. Thus in 1961, under the "Hawk Monaco" nomenclature, Stevens began work on a restyled version of the apparently timeless Studebaker coupe. Corresponding with this project was an assignment to Raymond Loewy to develop the Avanti. Both end products are worthy of all the praise that has been directed toward them. They were also the last examples of anything (save the Brooks Stevens' redesigned 1964 Larks) having even a semblance of newness to emerge from South Bend.

In less than a month, Stevens and his styling team created an automobile that blended the best of the original Bourke look, with a classic squared-off roofline and, via Mercedes-Benz influence, a refined interpretation of the original Hawk grille. In the process the now out-of-date tail fins were eliminated, helping

The Sceptre's roof and rear window lines foreshadowed the 1968 Chevrolet Impala's very similar treatment. Brooks Stevens photo.

This photo of Brooks Stevens' GT Hawk mock-up clearly shows the tacked-on nature of the new roof line. BROOKS STEVENS PHOTO

to impart to the Gran Turismo Hawk (as it was known in 1962) a timeless appeal. GT Hawks still look as good today as they did nearly 20 years ago.

The brilliance of Stevens' design was not only, however, founded on its outstanding appearance. On a budget that would have reminded GM's styling boss Williams of a bad joke, Stevens had no choice but to use every economy trick in the book. In essence, with the exception of the new roofline, the change in personality Stevens wrought was accomplished via the clever and tasteful redesign of trim items. Certainly not the least praiseworthy end product of Stevens' efforts was the Hawk's new dash, which he developed around a three-plane format. This approach, which was later adopted by both General Motors and Chrysler, remains to this day one of the best examples of how to properly lay out the instruments of an automobile. "For the man who really enjoys driving," *Car Life* (May, 1962) commented, "the Hawk has one of the most attractive and functional cockpits of any automobile built in this country."

No one, even Stevens, expected Egbert to unveil the new Hawk in September, 1962, but that was his intention. No small part of this minor miracle was played by Gene Hardig, Studebaker's long time chassis engineer.

Hawk sales responded well to Stevens' rejuvenation formula, rebounding from 3,929 in 1961 to 9,325 the following year. This was hardly enough to make Studebaker a sales threat to Chevrolet or anyone else. However, the accompanying publicity all Studebaker products received as a spin-off from this interest in the new Hawk must surely have been worth every penny Egbert paid Stevens for his services.

Car Life, which found many other features of the GT Hawk to its liking, was less than ecstatic about its braking capability. Indeed the *Car Life* testers managed to complete just one 80mph to

zero deacceleration run with the Hawk. At 20 mph, the Hawk's brakes had completely faded and its occupants had to occupy themselves as best they could as the car gradually coasted to a stop. As expected, when this test report was published, it generated a good deal of controversy among Studebaker supporters. Some rejected the accuracy of the test results and others noted that perhaps the non-standard full-width wheel covers installed on the Hawk were to blame, since they prevented air from reaching the drums. It is quite feasible that they were the culprits, since throughout the years the Hawk's finned brake drums had been the subject of considerable praise from numerous automotive journals.

Changes made in the appearance of the 1963 Hawk were minimal; mesh inserts in the front side grilles, circular amber parking lights, and a new red, white, and blue logo placed on the Hawk's doors and front grille being the most obvious changes. Both in 1963 and 1964, the Gran Turismo Hawks also were distinguished by their painted headlight rims. All earlier models were fitted with chrome rims.

The GT Hawk's new dash exemplified readability and simplicity. BROOKS STEVENS PHOTO

Both the Hawk and the Lark benefited substantially from the backwash of the Avanti performance development program. On April 15, 1963, Studebaker announced the availablity of new high-performance Hawk and Lark models known simply as the Super Hawk and Super Lark.

The extent of the changes made in the basic Hawk to transform it into a Super Hawk were rather extensive. With a price tag of $581.70, the Super Hawk package included the R-2 supercharged engine, power front disc brakes, front and rear heavy-duty shocks and springs, rear axle traction bars, a rear anti-roll bar, Twin-Traction limited-slip rear axle, 6.70 x 15 four-ply tires, a tachometer, and front and rear carpeting. The same list of options with the R-1 unsupercharged engine retailed for $371.70. The Super Hawk had to be ordered either with the four-speed manual transmission or the high performance Power-Shift automatic transmission

which allowed the driver to manually control its shifting.

There were also several cosmetic changes made to identify the Super Hawk, such as a speedometer reading to 160mph (normal GT Hawks had units measuring only up to 120mph), grille badges reading either "R-1" or "R-2", and, on the lower front fenders red, white, and blue identification bars with either an "Avanti powered" (R-1) or "Avanti supercharged" (R-2) script.

The R-2 engine, via a 9.0:1 compression ratio, four-barrel carburetor, and a Paxton SN-60 supercharger, developed approximately 300 horsepower. With the Power-Shift transmission, this was sufficient to move the Super Hawk from zero to 60 mph in 8.5 seconds. The Super Hawk's top-end potential was demonstrated by Andy Granatelli at the Bonneville Salt Flats, where in January, 1963, he was clocked through the flying mile at 140.23mph.

It was appropriate in a historical sense that a number of GT Hawks were among the 108 Studebakers built at South Bend on the last day the plant operated, December 20, 1963. In a sense, the last era of Studebaker history began in 1953 when the coupe was first produced. While Studebaker made numerous attempts after that date to reassert itself in the industry, 1953 was the last time it marketed automobiles that broke dramatically with the past. If Studebaker could have survived as a U.S. producer, the chances are good that a new Hawk would have been part of the Studebaker lineup. Brooks Stevens' prototype for such a car speaks for itself. Nevertheless the Hawk died on December 20, 1963. In retrospect it was a car initially ahead of its time and then, in spite of its many merits, never quite able to achieve the popularity many industry analysts believed it deserved.

GT Hawk upholstery echoed the rolled and pleated idiom. BROOKS STEVENS PHOTO

Here our Golden Hawk test car is off to the proving grounds.   Performance figures we obtained were startling to say the least.

STUDEBAKER'S

**All of our testers agreed on this one—
it's the sports-type car to beat for '56, from every standpoint.**

Over-all handling was fine, even above usual Studebaker standards. The Hawk understeers, has good correction control and fine brakes.

Dashboard is completely outfitted with Stewart-Warner instruments set into coined metal.   Note big tach on right.

WHEN ONE THINKS of a hawk there is usually an immediate association with three things—grace, speed and determination of purpose. Someone at Studebaker had what may well turn out to be the best automotive selling idea of the year when he thought to call his company's latest sports-type car the "Hawk" line. Whoever he was, he must have driven the cars first, because the name is a fitting one indeed. The Golden Hawk, in particular, is one of the fastest and best looking cars ever made on these shores. As for determination of purpose, you might even go so far as to call this a car of prey because it is going out after the Thunderbird, Corvette, Chrysler "300" market with a vengeance.

What is it like to drive the Golden Hawk? We'll get to that, but let's take a close look at it first. Outwardly, it is more than strongly reminiscent of last year's Studebaker Speedster, the major styling changes being a built-up, very Italian-looking and very handsome front grille and larger, higher rear fenders leading into a squared-off trunk lid, also with a grille effect. A long chrome strip from the head-light on either side all the way to the end of the car is deeply Veed just behind the rear window and we are told that the owner's initials may be placed in the V. In any event, the chrome also serves as a lovely separation for the two tones of paint. Frankly, we don't much care who gets the credit for this styling job, but we have always considered the basic Loewy Studebaker hardtops and coupes to be the most beautiful American body designs since the early Classic days, and the Hawk series is the best yet.

On the inside, the new "closer to Europe" theme has been carried through nobly. The dashboard is of coined metal with a real custom look and instrumentation by Stewart-Warner is complete even to a vacuum gauge, a tachometer and a clock with a sweep-second hand. All dials are large, completely calibrated and easy to read at a glance. Nor has safety been overlooked. Standard equipment includes two crash panels —one on the dash and the other behind the front seat—and safety door latches. Seat belts are optional.

Seating position is excellent; steering-wheel angle is just right and all the floor pedals come easily to foot, as the British might say. Visibility is excellent, even without a fishbowl windshield, and headroom is adequate unless you are a monster. Incidentally, the "old-fashioned" windshield makes entry and exit easier than in almost any other 1956 American car, in spite of the fact that the Golden Hawk is only a fraction over 56 inches high.

Getting in and out of the rear seats is a little more of a problem, but really no more so than in any two-door coupe, and anyone who complains about a scarcity of leg room doesn't deserve to own either a Golden Hawk or a Continental Mark II—or any other specialized machine. At that, there is actually plenty of room for two people on a long trip.

By the time we had discovered all of this we were fairly itching to drive the car, and since we were at the Studebaker proving grounds at South Bend, Indiana, we did just that. First came a feeling-out period on the long, winding country-type road they call Route 1. This is a sort of open-air torture chamber, with surfaces, grades and corners worse than you are apt to find in 10 years of CONTINUED ON PAGE 54

GOLDEN HAWK

AN AUTO AGE STAFF REPORT

ROAD AUTO AGE TEST

Here is the monster 275-hp power plant that gives the Golden Hawk its fantastic performance. The car's actual top speed is over 120 mph.

Golden Hawk does lean when cornered hard, but less than any other 5-passenger American automobile. It "tracks" well, never gets floppy.

Bill Holland

Studebaker Golden Hawk Specifications

Engine

Type: 90 V8
Valve Arrangement: In-head
Bore and stroke: 4 x 3½"
Displacement (cu in): 352
Cam ground (three-quarter)
Compression Ratio: 9.5-1
Taxable horsepower: 51.2
Advertised max brake horsepower
    at Engine Rpm: 275 @ 4600
Max torque (Ft lb @ rpm):
    380 @ 2800
Carburetor: 4-barrel, downdraft
Exhaust: Dual

Capacity

Oil: 5 quarts
Water (heater): 26.5 quarts
    (without heater): 25 quarts
Gas: 18 gallons

General

Wheelbase: 120.5 inches
Overall length: 203.9 inches
Overall width: 70.4 inches
Overall height: 56.3 inches
Tread front: 56.36 inches
    rear: 55.6 inches
Tires: Tubeless, 7.10 x 15

A great race driver and former Indy

winner gives his opinion of the leader

of the first line of sports cars in America

tests:

Studebaker

GOLDEN HAWK

By BILL HOLLAND

THIS WORLD IS BECOMING quite a confusing place for racing drivers like me. Just a short time ago there were only two kinds of cars as far as I was concerned—the racing car and the passenger car. It was very easy to tell them apart because one was an ultra-fast, stark or almost ugly single-seater and the other was a large, beautifully styled and sedate vehicle that would carry five or six people in complete comfort. "Never the twain shall meet," I thought.

Studebaker has proved I was wrong. Their new Golden Hawk is faster than many race cars, wonderful to look at and roomy enough to carry the whole family. This car is the lead model in a special four-model line of sports-type cars, the first, as far as I know, line of such cars to be introduced by an American auto maker.

Late in September, 1955, I was lucky enough to become the first person, other than a Studebaker engineer, to drive the Golden Hawk. It was in Detroit, on the fast, banked track on the Studebaker-Packard proving grounds. With many hundreds of miles of racing on the

Indianapolis track behind me I felt completely at home on the big two-and-a-half mile oval so I climbed into the Stude and charged right off.

I was impressed immediately with the tremendous acceleration of the car. Floor-boarded, it took off with hardly a trace of wheel spin and roared with turbine-like smoothness well up over the 100-mph mark without any lag or "flat spots" at all. Round and round I went and the speedometer needle slid easily past the 125-mph mark.

Finally I came in and checked with the engineers who had been timing me. I was delighted, but not at all surprised to find that the Golden Hawk had done two laps at an average of 121.0 miles per hour on the rain-soaked track. I told them I was impressed. It was an understatement.

Some weeks later, SPEED AGE asked me to go out to the Studebaker proving grounds in South Bend, Ind., to give the Golden Hawk a more thorough workout. Here I was able to run accurate acceleration and braking tests and I got to drive the car over a great variety

The 275-horsepower V-8 engine gives the Golden Hawk the highest horsepower to weight ratio of any volume-built U. S. car.

This front end view of the completely new Golden Hawk shows the daring grille and sweeping combination of foreign and U.S. lines.

of road surfaces. Here's what I found.

My original impression about the acceleration was easily confirmed. The Golden Hawk is absolutely breathtaking in acceleration, either from a standing start or from any cruising speed up to 80 or 90 miles per hour. From zero to 60 mph took just 9.6 seconds and the car needed only six seconds to go from 30 to 60 mph. That's about 20 per cent faster than the average fast sedan. These figures were gotten with a car equipped with the 1956 Packard Ultramatic transmission. Most of the Golden Hawks will be deliv-

ered with this automatic setup, but a manual three-speed shift and overdrive is also to be made available. You should be able to get even better performance, shifting by hand, and the overdrive will more than likely improve gas mileage if that's what you're interested in.

You may be wondering whether or not the car is hard to drive, or even if it's safe. I will say definitely that this automobile is not a compromise in any way between safety and performance. The power steering is light in operation and not geared too fast for average reflexes, and the new finned brakes

are especially good. The seating position is such that you are always completely relaxed and yet alert, and visibility is excellent all around.

Just under five feet in height, the car has a center of gravity so low that it would be almost impossible to turn it over. I put it through several controlled slides and found it recovered perfectly. It is balanced properly so that it can still be controlled with the steering wheel while it is sliding. This technique will be necessary only in an emergency, of course, but it's nice to know that your car is

Looking at the west end of the GH going east reveals a new concept in rear design. Over fender fins and squared trunk are among the attractions. Notice dual exhausts.

Dashboard incorporates a tachometer and vacuum gauge in addition to standard instruments. Standard safety equipment includes the crash pads for the panel, padding on the back of the front seat.

up to any situation that might arise.

I took the Stude over some bumpy, windy, hilly roads on the test grounds and found that I never once had to "fight" it. The ride is somewhat firmer than on previous Studebaker hardtops, but even on the worst bumps at high speed it never becomes harsh. That roof looks awfully low, but you soon learn that you don't have to worry about banging your head on it.

By now you may have gotten the impression that I like the car. I won't be at all guarded in my opinions; I like it very much. It has all

the power anyone could want, and then some—275-horsepower to be exact. In design, all the Hawk line is in sharp contrast to Studebaker's big new styling of its President, Commander and Champion series. The Golden Hawk is long and low and very sporty, and yet it has none of the disadvantages of the usual sports car. There is an excellent heater and defroster system, a fine radio, plenty of space for luggage and no service problem. Interior finishing is very attractive and the dashboard has enough instruments to satisfy an engineer, including a tachometer and a vacu-

um gauge. Seats are all extremely comfortable and so is the price— factory list $2800.00. Other models in the line step down in price and aim at combining performance with economy. The Sky Hawk has 210-horsepower V8, the Power Hawk 170-horsepower V8 engine, and the Flight Hawk has a 101-horsepower six-cylinder engine.

When you see your first Golden Hawk on the road, take a good, close look at the driver; it might be me. And I wouldn't be surprised if the second one you saw had another familiar face behind the wheel—your own.   ●

CAR LIFE CONSUMER ANALYSIS:

1956 golden hawk

Specifications

Model	Golden Hawk
Wheelbase	120½"
Length	204"
Engine Displacement	352 cu. in.
Bore & Stroke	4" x 3½"
Compression Ratio	9.5:1
Brake Horsepower	275
Torque	380 ft. lbs. at 2800
Electrical system	12 volt
Factory Price, without accessories	$3057

STUDEBAKER GOLDEN HAWK

THE STUDEBAKER GOLDEN HAWK heads a new series of 1956. Actually the four-car series includes the basic 120-inch wheelbase, five-passenger sports coupe with body design by Raymond Loewy, with 4 different engines.

For 1956, however, the original Loewy design (much bespangled with chrome in years past) has received a thoroughgoing face lift. The front end has been cleaned up and a higher hood with an egg-crate grille has replaced the sharply sloping nose. The rear deck has been redesigned to increase luggage space.

The four series, which can be distinguished only by nameplates and small differences in trim are: Golden Hawk with 275 bhp V8, Sky Hawk with 210 bhp V8, Power Hawk with 170 bhp V8 (optional power kit offers 185 bhp), and Flight Hawk with the 101 bhp Champion L-head 6-cylinder engine.

The Hawk might be called a "semi-sports car." It has some of the prerequisites of a sports machine, combined with all comforts and amenities of a luxury passenger car. Low center of gravity and very favorable power-to-weight ratio plus 380 ft. lbs. of torque at fairly low rpms could give some people the idea that they had a sports car on their hands. A professional or intelligent amateur soon realizes that the Hawk is better suited to high-speed touring work.

Primarily the Hawk's trouble is weight distribution. The car is heavy on the front end, which results in tendency for rear wheel slide on dry pavement.

The powerful, well-built engine on the Golden Hawk provides more power than the chassis design can properly

handle. A full-throttle start in reduced "D" range spins the rear wheels on dry pavement and keeps the tires screaming on the concrete up to 25 mph.

These troubles could be remedied to some extent by filling the trunk with sand bags, which would equalize the weight distribution and cut down the slide and wheel spin. Perhaps the best solution is to buy the lower-priced Sky Hawk with its lighter weight Studebaker V8 of 210 bhp.

The Hawk's low center of gravity makes for a fairly stable chassis with little or no roll, and gives the driver (especially if he's snugly belted in) the impression that he can corner on rails. Herein lies the car's built-in calamity factor; a novice driver might be lured into a fast corner by the Hawk's low CG and taut springing, and the rear end will break loose (although tire scream should give some warning on dry hard surfaces).

Used in its proper context as a fast touring car, however, the Hawk can win a host of friends. The new super highways, with their gentle, long-radius curves and open vistas, permit Hawk owners to devour miles at the rate of one every 45 or 50 seconds.

At the legal speeds the Hawk gives a very comfortable, extremely stable ride with swaying and pitching virtually eliminated. The chassis suspension and cushioning soak up all but the sharpest of surface roughness (cobblestones etc.).

The Hawk's instrument panel is excellent, but there should be a light for the transmission control quadrant. Panel has red sweep-second hand clock for timing and good instrument lighting except for colorful vacuum gauge which

YOUR CHECK LIST

☑ ☑ ☑ ☑ ☑ means top rating

PERFORMANCE ☑ ☑ ☑ ☑ ☑

Tops all other stock passenger cars with 275 bhp Packard V8 in lightweight coupe body. Will accelerate from 0 to 60 mph in a bit over 9 seconds. Top speed is 110 plus. Overdrive transmission recommended for best combination of performance and economy. Standard three-speed transmission without overdrive is not available.

STYLING ☑ ☑ ☑ ☑ ☐

Basically very pleasing. A good rework of the original Loewy design. There are two out-of-place details: 1) protruding dummy airscoop which clutters the hood lines, and 2) the dummy brake cooling intake which breaks up the body lines at the rear fender.

RIDING COMFORT ☑ ☑ ☑ ☑ ☑

Gets top rating in comparison to the other "sports type" cars, Corvette and Thunderbird. However, the overall ride is a bit firmer than the average passenger car. There is a welcome absence of swaying, rolling and pitching.

INTERIOR DESIGN ☑ ☑ ☑ ☑ ☐

Very good. Hawk has exceptional headroom for such a low-slung car with its low overall height. Front seat is easy to get in and out of and there is no blocking wraparound windshield extension. The rear seat is surprisingly roomy and comfortable for two adults, but entrance and exit require agility.

ROADABILITY ☑ ☑ ☑ ☑ ☐

Excellent when compared with other five- and six-passenger cars, but falls behind the two other semi-sports cars, Corvette and Thunderbird. Has good stability at high speed on rough surfaces but tends to spin out when pushed into sharp curves at excessive speed.

EASE OF CONTROL ☑ ☑ ☑ ☑ ☐

Heavy Packard engine makes power steering a must item. With it the car handles easily but wheel takes far too much winding. Road sense is a bit lacking at high speeds.

ECONOMY ☑ ☑ ☑ ☑ ☐

If driven conservatively, which seems unlikely in the case of most owners, it will deliver excellent gasoline mileage due to the low rear axle ratio with Ultramatic or overdrive.

SERVICEABILITY ☑ ☑ ☑ ☐ ☐

The big Packard V8 and all accessories make a close-packed jumble under the low-slung hood and a trial for even the most patient mechanic.

WORKMANSHIP ☑ ☑ ☑ ☑ ☐

Generally on a high level. When first introduced, the Studebaker sport coupes were a bit flimsy and "tinny" but small annoyances have been corrected. Paint, exterior trim and fitting of panels are good. Upholstery and interior trim are good.

DURABILITY ☑ ☑ ☑ ☐ ☐

Appears satisfactory on new car, but just how well the light body and frame structure will stand up under severe treatment remains an unknown factor at this time.

VALUE PER DOLLAR ☑ ☑ ☑ ☐ ☐

Although the Studebaker sports coupes have had high depreciation in the past, it is too early to predict how the new Hawk versions will fare. For a fast sports touring coupe, the lower-powered, lower-priced Sky Hawk and Power Hawks will probably be better values over long-term ownership.

is a bit too brilliant on high lighting. The panel lights could use a rheostat. Vision out the windshield is excellent, with a view over the sloping hood at both fenders. Corner posts at left and the wide frame of the ventilator and window make a more noticeable dead spot because the seating position puts you so close to them.

Familiar Studebaker underseat "Climitizer" heating system works well, dispels drafts, but pours most of the heated air on the right hand side of the car. This can be offset somewhat by opening front window a crack at left side of car and letting the slight pressure of the system do the rest.

Upholstery is durable, well-tailored Naugahyde and the attractive, perforated plastic roof liner and insulation, close to the steel, allows a surprising amount of headroom. A tall, 6-foot-plus driver can wear a high-crowned felt hat. Seating position is good with wheel located low and in your lap.

Seats are well-upholstered and comfortable. Exterior styling is generally good, if a bit on the cluttered side, with totally unnecessary dummy air intake breaking the smooth hoodline. The simple grille is pleasing but may cause people to nickname the Hawks "South Bend Ferraris."

Brakes are good, and they can lock the wheels if need be, but on low-mileage test car they had a tendency to grab and swerve the car unless applied with care.

Summing up: A stylish, roomy and comfortable (for five passengers) sports coupe with more than average sedan stability coupled with a terrific power plant that provides more performance than the car is capable of using efficiently.

New Sports-type
STUDEBAKER HAWK
is supercharged...

Variable rate suspension on all models

The Studebaker range for 1957 is headed by the advance-styled Golden Hawk, which features a centrifugal supercharger, non-slip power dividing differential, 15 per cent better performance, 20 per cent quicker steering, and many new safety items.

THE sleek, stylish "Golden Hawk" with new supercharged 275 h.p. V-8 engine, new front-rear weight distribution, and the most favourable power-to-weight ratio in its class, will be the highest performance U.S. car in its price field for 1957, says Studebaker engineers. It is the only American car featuring a supercharger as standard equipment.

The new Hawk range includes the lower priced "Silver Hawk" V-8 with 210 h.p. engine (225 h.p. with optional power kit), and the "Silver Hawk Six" with economical 101 h.p. in-line engine. All cars feature advanced sports styling with canted rear fender fins.

The long, low Hawks with their smart European look are in sharp contrast to Studebaker's standard line of more orthodox family sedans and station wagons.

The "Golden Hawk's" low-pressure supercharger is driven through a belt and variable rate pulley, and produces five pounds of boost throughout the car's driving range. Maximum accelerative power is claimed, while normal economy at cruising speed is not affected. Acceleration times stated are: 0 to 60, using the "Flightomatic" torque converter transmission, 9.0.: 30-60, 5.0s.

New improvements are: optional power braking, steering, seats, and windows; dual exhausts; finned brake drums; safety type steering wheel. The "Golden Hawk" bonnet has a fibre glass overlay. Two tone exteriors are standard, with harmonising gold vinyl upholstery optional at no extra cost.

Studebaker's sedan range of 15 models in three series has moved into the big car class, the "President Classic's" 120½" wheelbase being the longest in the U.S. low-price field. All sedans for 1957 are fitted with Studebaker's "Luxury-Level" ride with variable rate coil springing, and the "Twin Traction" non-slip power dividing differential. Both innovations are American stock "firsts."

Finned brake drums, safety steering wheel, two-speed electric windshield wipers, and hill-holders are fitted as standard, as well as several other safety features such as padded dashboards.

Overdrive and "Flightomatic" transmission are optional on all models, and economy is said to be good. ●

Main differences between "Golden Hawk" and "Silver Hawk" (pictured) are the wheels and top of bonnet. Car has 210 h.p. V8 engine.

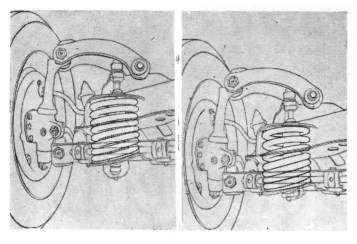

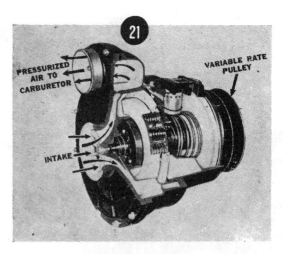

Conventional front coil spring. New variable rate front coil spring.

Picture shows how new Studebaker variable rate springing automatically compensates for varying loads, ensuring a soft, comfortable ride. Car is said to corner better, and driver to maintain better control.

"Golden Hawk's" supercharger is belt-driven through a variable rate pulley, delivers five pounds of boost. Pressurised induction gives the car the highest h.p.-per-cu.-in. of any U.S. car in its class.

New Studebaker "Golden Hawk" is a 5-passenger hardtop only 56" high, but 17 feet long. It has a 275 h.p. V8 engine, with supercharger as standard equipment. Quicker steering, better acceleration and weight distribution, non-slip power dividing diff., dual exhausts, tachometer, finned brake drums are outstanding features. Styling is Continental inspired.

1957 Studebaker "President Classic" . . . longer, lower, safer — and just as economical as previous models.

Bob Veith

TESTS AND COMPARES:

CORVETTE
T-BIRD
GOLDEN

Bob Veith, this month's comparison tester, is one of the fastest-rising stars along the Championship Trail. Last year he drove the Federal Engineering Special to seventh place at Indianapolis and won the coveted Stark & Wetzel Rookie of the Year Award.

This year's versions of Detroit's
hot trio have one thing in common—GO!
Here's how they stack up comparatively.

By BOB VEITH

MY STRONGEST impression after comparison-testing the 1957 Ford Thunderbird, Studebaker Golden Hawk and Chevrolet Corvette is that they're geared for go! All three of these American-built sports-type cars are virtual bombs, loaded with power; yet characterized by individual styling and performance features that set one aside from the other.

I doubt seriously if any of them can be classed as true sports cars for, in most cases, they have been designed to achieve more than one purpose. The Golden Hawk, for instance, obviously was designed for family-car comfort and roominess with sports car performance added. The Thunderbird meets the situation about half-way in each direction. It looks a great deal like a sports car, contains many sports car features, and yet has the soft ride and other features of a family car. As for the Corvette, it undoubtedly has been styled to appeal to sports car enthusiasts, and its designers have gone all out to make the Corvette a true sports car.

In my recent test of these cars, made exclusively for SPEED AGE, I found them all to my liking, with the exception of various individual characteristics which we shall discuss throughout the story. In any case, there is no doubt-ing that each of these cars have been designed to fill a particular purpose, according to the wants of the public.

There were many individual differences on each of our test cars to make a true comparison somewhat difficult, and these things should be kept in mind. The Thunderbird, for instance, was the only one of the three to be equipped with power accessories. It featured Ford's power brakes and steering while the others were standard. Then too, the Bird used in our test had a single four-throat carburetor whereas the Corvette was equipped with twin quads and the Hawk featured a belt-driven McCulloch supercharger which is standard on the '57. In addition, the Bird and Corvette were equipped with automatic transmissions while the Hawk had a stick shift and overdrive.

How did they stack up against each other? Well . . . let's take them apart step by step and see.

Designwise, there hasn't been a great deal of change in any of the three cars over last year's models. Hardly any change at all is noticeable in the appearance of the '57 Corvette over the '56, and the same holds true for the T-Bird; although the latter does boast a slight change to the rear deck and bumper. Hawk body changes include canted tail fins which are a big improvement; louvering of the hood; a bit less chrome stripping; and redesigned tail

HAWK

Corvette shows very little styling change, but the new power plant is loaded with high-speed punch.

lights. In each case, the three cars have retained the basic body styles that have become so familiar to today's motorist.

THE CORVETTE

For the out-and-out sports car enthusiast, the '57 Corvette has the best styling and comes closest to filling the bill for a true sports car—even to the simulated wheel hubs, which are most realistic. Bucket seats, stiff shocking, lack of bulky bumpers on both front and rear, plus a moderate use of chrome stripping add a racy look to the car, and give it the feel of a true sports car.

The Corvette is small, with a 102-inch wheelbase and an overall height of 49.2 inches with the convertible soft top down. A removable metal top also is available, which extends the overall height to 51 inches. Twin exhausts, projecting from the rear fenders, offer a pleasant rumble that goes naturally with the car's racy design.

The body is made of fiberglass and is comparatively light. Workmanship seems better than in previous years, but I cannot understand why the designers persisted in using fiberglass for the firewall separating the engine compartment from the cockpit. Any car that is likely to be used in competition, such as the Corvette, should have the safety of a solid metal firewall to protect the driver in the event of trouble.

Fuel injection, of course, is a new feature with the stock Chevrolet as well as the Corvette, and with it the senior engine in the Corvette line boasts one horsepower for each cubic inch of piston displacement. This big engine is listed at 283 cubic inches with an identical horsepower rating. Our test car, however, contained the 245 hp V-8 power plant, equipped with twin four-throat carburetors. A 220 hp engine with single quad carburetion also is available.

Like most sports cars, the Corvette is a bit difficult to get in and out of, especially for a big man like myself, but I soon acquired the knack and didn't have much trouble after awhile. Inside, leg room is surprisingly plentiful and I went for the bucket seats. They seemed to offer me more support, especially to my back and legs. The interior itself is luxurious, with foam rubber cushioning and leather upholstery matched in color with the floor carpeting.

The steering wheel of the Corvette definitely is of sports car design, and sits at a comfortable angle which offers the best possible vision through the wraparound windshield. The seat adjustment, however, is limited. I would suggest an adjustable steering column that would help solve the problem for big fellows like me.

Our test Corvette was equipped with safety belts, but these are optional, as they are on the T-Bird and Golden Hawk. I can't see why belts are not standard equipment,

Front-rear views show T-Bird to be noticeably lower. Continent-style spare mounting has been replaced by trunk stowage, as in earliest models.

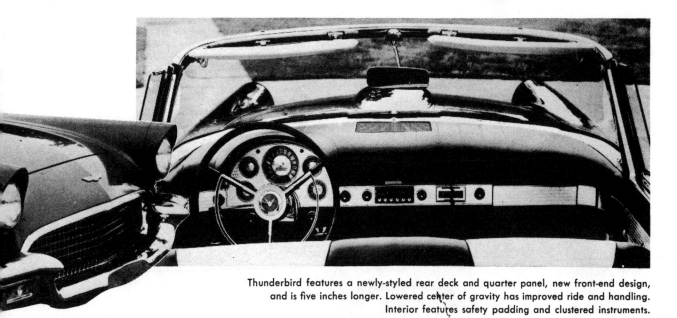

Thunderbird features a newly-styled rear deck and quarter panel, new front-end design, and is five inches longer. Lowered center of gravity has improved ride and handling. Interior features safety padding and clustered instruments.

especially on cars such as these, which are designed for sports-minded enthusiasts. I don't believe the public will ever use seat belts religiously unless the manufacturers push them harder. Many people do use them now, but I'm for making them standard equipment.

While the Corvette was equipped with just about every necessary instrument and gauge, including a tachometer, the instrument panel is not laid out practically. The tach and speedometer can be read without difficulty; but some of the important gauges, such as the oil pressure and ammeter, are strung out far to the right of the driver. I was hunting and taking my eyes off the road for too long a period to see them.

Forward vision out of the wraparound windshield is good; but side vision is restricted with the top up. I found it difficult to see oncoming traffic when pulling onto a main highway from a side road. This problem, of course, does not exist when the top is removed. Unfortunately, our test was made in the rain, so the top was most welcome at the time.

Also in the sports car style is the Corvette's gear shift or selector—a stubby lever located on the floor within easy reach of the driver's right hand. It was no problem to select the proper gear without hunting—a problem I had with the Thunderbird.

As for performance and handling, I could sense the Corvette's power before I even started away from the curb for the first time. It took off with a neck-snapping burst that promised an interesting time in the acceleration runs I was to make later on the drag strip at Long Beach, California.

As mentioned, it was raining when I put the Corvette through its paces; but despite wet pavement it accelerated with tremendous punch. Equipped with a 3.55 gear, we took the car through a series of runs on the drag strip. Surprisingly enough, there wasn't much rear-wheel slippage from the wet pavement during any of the runs. The engine never missed a beat. It seemed willing and capable of taking every bit of throttle I gave it, and the higher the tach went the more punch it delivered. Here are the figures:

0-30	0-40	0-50	0-60	0-90	0-100
2.82	4.24	5.21	6.93	15.50	17.59

From 30 mph on up, the engine seemed to deliver more punch, and continued to do so as the speed soared. Actually there was some slippage at higher speeds, which might have held our 0-100 test down somewhat. But the figures we did come up with are indicative of the wallop the car has. Most of the runs were made in low gear, shifting into drive when necessary on the longer runs. Our figures came out much better this way, since there was a slight miss

Golden Hawk is a family-size car, the only one of the "hot trio" with a rear seat. A supercharger (right) is standard equipment on the 275-hp engine, yielding impressive acceleration in lower speed ranges.

noticeable when we tried accelerating in drive range.

These acceleration runs also provide a good brake test since I brought the car to an immediate stop after each run. The best test came from our 0-100 run when I brought the Corvette to a panic stop. There was considerable brake fade under constant usage, but our panic stop wound up without incident.

Handling and cornering, the Corvette was a bit light on the rear end. I took it over a winding course of twisting left and right hand turns running uphill and down. The car handled well, but it seemed stiffer shocked than the '56, and gave a more jarring ride. There wasn't much body lean as I bent it into tight turns, but the back end wanted to get out.

Taking it into a turn, the car felt stable until I began punching the throttle for quick acceleration coming out. Too much punch broke the rear wheels loose from the pavement and caused the back end to sway. When that happened, I was forced to get off the throttle for an instant in order to correct the drift. A bit more weight, perhaps by moving the engine back slightly, might have corrected this.

Steering was about right. It was fast; but not too fast so as to cause oversteering in the turns. Whenever I did get into a slide, a slight turn of the wheel brought me out of it without a lot of effort. Then, too, the engine picked up rpm in a hurry. Much better, in fact, than last year's Corvette. What rpm I lost in backing off to correct a slide was quickly regained, so I didn't lose much time in the corners.

Generally speaking, I'd say that the Corvette has come a long way in the American-built sports car picture since it was first introduced to the public. Its future then was uncertain, but the '57 certainly dispels any doubts that the Corvette is here to stay.

THE THUNDERBIRD

The '57 Thunderbird, although not emphasizing true sports car design to the extreme of the Corvette, carries many sports car characteristics. Like the Corvette, it is small, with a 102-inch wheelbase and a 51.6-inch overall height with removable hard top. But still it carries the comfort and many other features of a passenger car, such as a solid seat and softer shocking.

The T-Bird's bumpers, highly chromed and rather large, are related to a passenger car; but the famous Thunderbird grille work and sculptured rear fins give it the look of a sleek sports model. I thought the fins and grilles really emphasize the Bird's good looks.

Luggage space in the '57 is greater than before, even with the spare tire now located inside. However there is no solid partition between the inside end of the trunk and rear of the seats. With the car's top down, a person could simply open the door, reach behind the seat, and remove whatever was locked in the trunk. The only partition on our test car was a cloth which separated the trunk from the back of the seat.

Like the Corvette, the Thunderbird also has a removable metal top as well as a convertible soft top for foul-

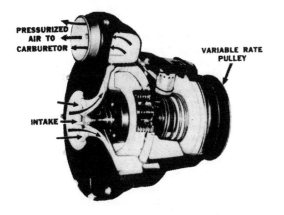

COMPARATIVE SPECIFICATIONS

1957	CORVETTE	T-BIRD	HAWK
ENGINE:			
CYLINDERS	V-8	V-8	V-8
BORE	3.875	3.80	3.56
STROKE	3.00	3.44	3.63
DISPLACE-MENT	283 CU. IN.	312 CU. IN.	289 CU. IN.
COMPRES-SION RATIO	9.5:1	9.7:1	7.8:1
MAXIMUM HP	245 a 5000	245 a 4500	275 a 4800
MAXIMUM TORQUE	300 LB/FT @ 3800	332 LB/FT a 3200	333 LB/FT a 3200
CARBURE-TION	TWIN QUADS	SINGLE QUAD	SINGLE DUAL-THROAT W SUPER-CHARGER
HP. PER CUBIC INCH	.866	.788	.951
GEARING:			
TRANSMIS-SION	POWERGLIDE	FORDOMATIC	STICK SHIFT W OVER-DRIVE
REAR	3.55	3.56	3.56
DIMENSIONS:			
WHEELBASE	102 IN.	102 IN.	120.5 IN.
LENGTH-OVERALL	168.01 IN.	181.4 IN.	204 IN.
WIDTH OVERALL	70.46 IN.	72.8 IN.	71.3 IN.
HEIGHT OVERALL	51.09 IN.	51.6 IN.	56.5 IN.
TREAD-FRONT	57 IN.	56 IN.	56.7 IN.
REAR	59 IN.	56 IN.	55.7 IN.
POWER-WEIGHT RATIO:			
WEIGHT	2829 LB.	3372 LB.	3265 LB.
POUNDS/HP	11.54 LB.	13.76 LB.	11.67 LB.
PERFORMANCE:			
TOP SPEED	122.5 MPH.	119.3 MPH.	127.5 MPH
ACCELERATION 0 - 30 MPH	2.82 SEC.	3.65 SEC.	2.63 SEC.
0 - 40	4.24	5.45	3.79
0 - 50	5.21	7.23	5.69
0 - 60	6.93	8.49	7.46
0 - 90	15.50	19.65	16.85
0 - 100	17.59	22.19	23.73

weather driving. Two metal tops, in fact, are available this year. The standard one is fitted with two "port" windows that offer better side vision. The other does not have the port holes and looks more attractive. So you have a choice of a top with better side vision or one that restricts side vision but looks nice.

A true padded dash is one of the finer points of the T-Bird's elaborate interior. Then, too, I liked the clustered instrument panel, hooded from glare and located directly in front of the driver for quick reading. It contained a tacho-meter, but I was disappointed by the absence of an oil pressure gauge and ammeter. Like passenger cars, the Thunderbird uses red warning lights for oil and battery. I much prefer the others, especially for a sports car design.

Leg room was a bit more cramped than in the Corvette, and I didn't feel quite as comfortable in the solid seat as I did in the bucket type. However I liked the way I could rest my right leg against the gear selector located on the floor. It was a restful position for long drives. The gear selector itself had a lock button located on top of the knob which eliminated the possibility of moving the selector from drive to reverse while in motion. This lock must be depressed before the lever can be moved out of "park" position or into reverse. It is a good point; but a little bothersome to work at times.

Seating position in the Bird is comfortable; but I found the seat adjustment limited, and there's a definite need for an adjustable steering-wheel column. The steering wheel itself is ideally located for comfort and good vision through the wrap-around windshield.

As mentioned, our test Thunderbird was powered by a 312-inch V-8 engine with a single quad carburetor and a horsepower rating of 245. It also had power brakes and steering which ate up some of that horsepower, but made for more comfortable driving. Other power plants available this year are the 312 inch 270 hp V-8 with twin quads, and the 292-inch 212 hp V-8 with a double barrel carburetor. Over-drive also is available with stick transmission. Our test car was equipped with Fordomatic drive, and a 3.56 gear.

Our test car was lively enough on the highway, but did not measure up to the acceleration of the Corvette. This was to be expected because of the difference in carburetion and engine size.

I used low range when possible on each of the acceleration tests, shifting into drive on the longer runs. The times we came up with were not as quick as the Corvette but we weren't exactly standing still, either. Any car that will accelerate from 0-60 in under nine seconds these days is fairly quick. Here are the results of the T-Bird runs:

0-30	0-40	0-50	0-60	0-90	0-100
3.65	5.45	7.23	8.49	19.65	22.19

The take-off response up to 70 mph was neck-snapping all right, and the engine continued to deliver a good punch even on the high end, all things considered. Our time from 0-100 was slow by comparison to the Corvette, but the engine was still revving at the end of our run. This meant it was capable of much more speed before starting to peak out.

Braking was rather severe on the Bird, on panic stops especially. There was noticeable fade under constant use but good recovery. Our power-brake panic stop was even, and we didn't do much fishtailing despite the wet pavement.

For handling and cornering, the Thunderbird gave its competitors a real run for their money. It felt to me the best balanced of the three, with even weight-distribution throughout to make cornering in tight turns a comparatively easy chore. High speed or low speed running, and even on slick pavement, it outhandled the others.

Most impressive was the way it laid into sharp corners. I could take it in hard, begin a desired four-wheel drift, then climb on the throttle and accelerate out of the turn in quick time. Shocking was softer than on the Corvette; but body lean and front-end dive

was hardly noticeable, since weight distribution seemed to allow an even four-wheel drift that kept both the front and back end stable.

I wasn't too keen on power steering, but the more I drove the Thunderbird through winding curves the better I liked it. It is quick and positive, with instant reaction to the slightest turn. Unlike conventional steering, it isn't necessary to lead the wheel or begin the turn before you actually get into it.

Although the Bird's acceleration figures were slower than the Corvette, the 245-hp engine moved out of the turns in a hurry whenever I stood on it during the cornering and handling tests. The power was always there when I needed it.

For the enthusiast who wants more rapid acceleration, the Thunderbird's 270 with dual quads should give him all the punch he wants. In any case, the '57 T-Bird stands to become more popular than ever before. Its soft and comfortable ride, plus its sport-car handling and good looks, are qualities that appeal to any red-blooded motorist.

THE GOLDEN HAWK

I give a lot of credit to Studebaker designers and engineers, who were faced with the problem of coming up with a dual-purpose automobile. It had to be big enough and appealing enough for the family man who also loved sports-car design and features. Their answer was the Golden Hawk.

Unlike the Thunderbird and Corvette, the Hawk was designed to fit a family man's needs as well as those of a sports car advocate. This meant the designing of a bigger and heavier automobile with the punch and looks of a sports model. The '57 Hawk has achieved this purpose with a well-designed five-passenger automobile powered with a 275 hp supercharged V-8 engine that packs a mean wallop.

Supercharging the '57 Hawk is one of the main selling points this year, but there have been other changes, too. The body style, for instance, is greatly improved over last year, with the canted fins, new style taillights and modest chrome stripping. Following the passenger car design, it has a solid roof that is not removable, but still the car has a sporting look about it.

The swept back roof, low silhouette, louvered hood and unmistakable snout-like grille give the Hawk a handsome look, and distinguish it from standard Studebaker models. Like the Corvette and T-Bird, it attracted plenty of attention from passing motorists and pedestrians, who stopped to look it over whenever we parked.

This year's Hawk has a 120.5-inch wheelbase plus new improved-action steering that is a great improvement

over last year's model. Improved shocks and longer springs give the car a smooth, easy ride. The instrument panel, although plain, is highly practical. Gauges include a tachometer, plus an oil pressure and amp gauge. The vacuum gauge helps in economy driving.

The Hawk's engine for '57 is of Studebaker design, and replaces the 275-hp Packard V-8 used in the '56 models. The new Jet Stream supercharger is standard equipment on all Golden Hawks this year, adding a tremendous thrust to the 289 cubin inch V-8 power plant. The blower is centrifugal-type, self-lubricating and comparatively quiet in operation.

Surprisingly enough, the exceptional gas mileage, for which Studebaker has been known, has not been lost with the addition of the blower.

We put the Hawk through acceleration runs over the Long Beach drag strip just as we had the Corvette and T-Bird. There was one difference: we had a dry day for the Hawk test. Our test car contained a 3.56 gear and a stick transmission. It didn't beat the Corvette at high speeds, but from 0-40 mph it was the fastest of the three. Here are those results:

0-30	0-40	0-50	0-60	0-90	0-100
2.63	3.79	5.69	7.46	16.85	23.73

The blower definitely gave the car a tremendous boost on acceleration, especially on the low end, as the comparison figures show. It was very effective up to 70 mph, when it began peaking out slightly. At 90 mph, the rpm really began running out, and we lost considerable elapsed time from 90 to 100. The figures show the Thunderbird, which was slower than the Hawk and Corvette in each of the other acceleration runs, was actually faster than the Hawk from 0-100 mph.

This peaking out at about 90 mph is a problem that the factory has been conscious of for some time now, and a modification that will correct it is being made available. Most of the trouble seems to lie in carburetion—possibly too small a carburetor bowl area. Several Hawk owners have helped the situation by adding an electric booster fuel pump or by installing a smaller carburetor float.

On acceleration, I experienced some rear end chatter caused by the rear wheels breaking traction. As in the Corvette, the rear end was light. Much of the Hawk's weight seems to be concentrated on the front wheels. This was noticeable in cornering and handling tests. I would prefer Traction Masters for more positive rear traction on acceleration, and heavier shocks and springs for handling. Heavy-duty shock absorbers and springs are available for the Hawk this year, as optional.

CONTINUED ON PAGE **68**

The 275 hp. GOLDEN HAWK

Most power-per-pound of any American car!

Zero to 60 mph. in 8.7 seconds . . . 60 to 100 mph. in 17.7 seconds! Torque, 380 ft./lbs. at 2800 rpm.; engine, 352 cu. in., V8, OHV; compression, 9.50 to 1; bore 4", stroke 3.50"; hydraulic valve action; dual exhausts; 4-barrel carburetion. Round-dial true sports instrumentation includes vacuum gauge and tachometer. Brake area, 195.3 sq. in.—biggest, safest braking-to-weight ratio of any car. Ultramatic Drive and all power assists available. Engineered to out-handle and out-run sports cars costing thousands more.

Room for 5 and a full size trunk!

Sweet and swift, safe and snug—that's a Hawk! Now you can have the sports performance you've always wanted and share the fun with family and friends. Four luxurious, 5-passenger Hawks to choose from, four price ranges—including the lowest. See them, drive them—get in on the fun—at your Studebaker Dealer's, today!

Tune in "TV Reader's Digest" every week.

Studebaker *Hawks*

GOLDEN HAWK
SKY HAWK
POWER HAWK
FLIGHT HAWK

Studebaker Division, Studebaker-Packard Corporation—Where pride of workmanship still comes first!

NEW CARS

Unusual two-colour zoning and "blisters" for the paired head lamps on the Studebaker President four-door saloon

1958 STUDEBAKER-PACKARD

Unusual for an American car is the almost entire absence of chromium on the Studebaker Scotsman

European influence is evident in the simple and restrained styling at the front of the Studebaker Golden Hawk. Side lamps are mounted separately above the front wings

Latest addition to the Studebaker range is this President hardtop. There is no centre pillar above the waist

PRODUCTS of the Studebaker-Packard Corporation for the 1958 season, examples of which were shown at the Paris Salon and the London Show at Earls Court, incorporate no major mechanical or bodywork changes, except that a modified version of the Studebaker Golden Hawk now bears the name of Packard, and is distinguished from the Studebaker by a steeply-sloping bonnet and full-width intake orifice.

Both cars have the same chassis dimensions, and the same supercharged vee-8 engine giving 275 b.h.p. The Packard version has pleated leather upholstery and other minor differences of trim and equipment. This is the only Packard model at present on the market.

Since the original announcement of the 1958 range, a new body has been introduced in the Studebaker Commander and President series. This is a two-door hardtop, reminiscent of the Hawk, with no centre pillar above the waist line. Overall height is 4ft 9½in.

The Studebaker range of sedans and station wagons comprises the Champion and Scotsman economy models having a 76.2 × 111.1 mm (3,041 c.c.) six-cylinder side-valve engine; the Commander four-door sedan and Provincial station wagon with a 4,248 c.c. vee-8 engine giving 180 b.h.p. (195 b.h.p. with the optional power kit of four-choke carburettor and dual exhausts); and the President four-door sedan which has a 225 b.h.p. vee-8 of 4,736 c.c.

Of the sporting Hawk line there are three versions—the Golden Hawk already referred to and the Silver Hawk, which can be had with either the side-valve engine as used in the Champion and Scotsman, or the larger vee-8 engine tuned for either 210 or 225 b.h.p.

The Hawk models and the President are mounted on a 10ft 0½in wheelbase, whereas all the others are shorter by 4in; 14in wheels have replaced 15in, and this, together with a one-piece propeller shaft to allow a lower floor level, has reduced the overall heights.

Dual head lamps are standard on the Commander and President series, optional on the Champions, and not available on the Hawks. Of these, the outer lamps are used for town driving and comprise also the dipped beam, whereas the inner lamps are set for full range and are cut when the dipper switch is pressed.

Variable-rate coil springs for the front suspension, leaf springs at the rear which

CONTINUED ON PAGE 54

STUDEBAKER LARK SPECIFICATION

Cylinders	Six	V-8
Bore	76.1 mm.	90.4 mm.
Stroke	101.5 mm.	82.5 mm.
Cubic capacity	2,785 c.c.	4,248 c.c.
Piston area	42.2 sq. in.	79.4 sq. in.
Valves	Side	pushrod o.h.v
Compression ratio ...	8.3	8.8
Max. power (gross) ...	90 b.h.p.	180 b.h.p.
at	4,000 r.p.m.	4,500 r.p.m.
Max. b.m.e.p.	129 lb./sq. in.	152 lb./sq. in.
at	2,000 r.p.m.	2,800 r.p.m.
Top-gear ratio (normal transmission) ...	3.54/1	3.31/1
Wheelbase	9 ft. 0½ in.	9 ft. 0½ in.
Overall length	14 ft. 6¾ in.	14 ft. 6¾ in.
Width	5 ft. 9 in.	5 ft. 9 in.
Height	4 ft. 9½ in.	4 ft. 9½ in.
Dry weight	23¼ cwt.	26½ cwt.
Turning circle	37½ ft.	37½ ft.
Brake lining area ...	147½ sq. in.	147½ sq. in.
Tyre size	5.90—15	6.40—15
Top gear m.p.h. at 1,000 r.p.m.	20.8	23.1
Top gear m.p.h. at 1,000 ft./min. piston speed	31.2	42.6

Neat and unadorned, the Lark which is seen here as the two-door hardtop model is America's most serious attempt yet to build a car that is economical in every way.

1959 CARS

The STUDEBAKER LARK

An American Small Car First Announced in *The Motor* Last Week

NEWS from the United States in recent months has made much of the public reaction said to be growing against a constant diet of Longer, Lower, Wider automobiles, a feeling which has so far been met by Detroit's Big Three exclusively with models which are yet Longer, still Lower and even Wider. If the public-opinion testers are correct a healthy revival should be in store for the Studebaker-Packard Corporation in their remote (from Detroit) fastness of South Bend, Indiana, which have been the first to take the plunge on models combining really compact size with very simple decoration.

The Lark series which is the fruit of this bold decision is evidently intended to offer the American public the possibility of all-round economy. Although passenger accommodation is claimed to be rather more liberal than last year, it is enclosed in a smaller body which is hence cheaper to build, less vulnerable to damage and easier to repair (having detachable wing panels), and deliberately undating, to suffer less by depreciation.

Considerable efforts have also been made to provide economical performance. The capacity of the six-cylinder side-valve engine supplied with the cheaper models has been reduced from 3,041 c.c. to a mere 2,785 c.c. by shortening the stroke, while at the same time a re-designed cylinder head allows an increase of compression ratio to 8.3/1 without sacrificing the ability to run on "regular-grade" fuel of about 90 Octane. The power output is given as 90 b.h.p. at 4,000 r.p.m.—the first new American model to have less than 100 b.h.p. for some years—and the maximum torque of 1,740 lb. in. occurs at half that engine speed. A new automatic-choke carburetter has been designed, with economy chiefly in view, in which the enrichment jet for maximum acceleration is opened only by a combination of vacuum and extreme throttle pedal movement. Plainly indicative of the way the company is thinking is the claim for a 20% improvement in torque and 8% improvement in economy at 35 *m.p.h.* For customers in search of performance there is a V-8 engine of 4,248 c.c. developing 180 b.h.p., or 195 b.h.p. when equipped with a four-choke carburetter and dual exhaust. Like the Six it is intended for 90 Octane fuel.

The styling ancestry of the Larks is evident from the Hawk series which is continued as the prestige car of the range, the silhouette being effectively that of the Loewy-designed "sports" models shorn once more of tail fins and drastically trimmed of front and rear overhang. The extent of the trimming can be judged from the comparative overall lengths: 14 ft. 7 in. for the Lark saloon, 17 ft. for the Hawk coupé. A typical family saloon from one of the Detroit Big Three is 14 in. longer still.

Studebaker have never lagged in technical progress, and although there are no outstanding engineering changes in the latest cars a large number of details have been improved to consolidate ground already won. Reduction in weight has led to redesigning of the variable-rate front coil-spring suspension, with new rear springs and modified shock absorbers. This, with a wider track, is said to reduce cornering roll, while the steering has been given a variable ratio to make it more direct, lighter and better at self-centring. Power brakes, a limited-slip differential and air-conditioning are available as extras on all models, as well as power steering on the V-8 cars. An automatic "hill-holder," which traps pressure in the brake system when the car stops on an upgrade, is offered as an option on all models except those with automatic transmission.

Like the Lark, the well-known Hawk model is available with either a 90 b.h.p., side-valve six-cylinder engine or a 180 b.h.p. V-8.

STUDEBAKER LARK

By JIM WHIPPLE

STUDEBAKER has pulled out of "across the board" competition with the auto industry's Big Three this year.

Instead, the onetime wagon works has made a clean end run into a new and highly promising field, the compact-economy low-priced group which Rambler's American "rediscovered" in 1958.

Studebaker's new Lark line is something unique in current American automotive history — a small, big car. Briefly, to establish its size relationship for you, it's 175 inches from bumper to bumper. That's just 14 inches longer than a Volkswagen. Its wheelbase however, is 108 inches, the same as that of the "big" Rambler and Rambler Rebel V-8s, which are 16 inches longer overall.

The result is a very ingenious package which Studebaker engineers have built around their full-sized passenger compartment designed to hold six people in comfort and space equal to that found in a Ford, Chevy or Plymouth.

What Studebaker did was to start with the 1958 Scotsman-Champion-Commander body understructure, or "shell", which last appeared on cars with 116½-inch wheelbase and 202-inch overall lengths, and design a new frame for it. This new frame, shorter but much stronger, cut the wheelbase by moving the front axle back 8 inches, and at the same time provided space for either the 170 cu. in. six cylinder or the 259 cu. in. V-8 engine. Then they finished the job with entirely new front and rear body sections.

The 27-inch reduction in overall length took place without sacrificing one inch from the passenger area or moving the rear wheels uncomfortably close to the rear seat. The new frame has permitted a slight lowering of the car with no sacrifice of generous headroom.

The only price that had to be paid for the almost two-and-one-half foot reduction in overall length and 300-lb. saving in dead weight, was about a seven inch cut in the length (front to rear) of the luggage compartment.

Studebaker designers went about shortening their Lark very simply.

They took their standard passenger compartment, kept the rear axle static in relationship to it and lopped off approximately 12 inches of rear overhang and 15 inches from the front end.

As a result the trunk is shorter and there is absolutely no waste space between front bumper and grille, grille and radiator, radiator and engine, and engine and firewall.

These are the facts and figures of the Lark — from them you get an idea of what Studebaker has done but nothing prepares you for the result.

The psychological effect of the car is remarkable. From the outside it looks cut, vaguely like several European imports such as its S-P stablemates the Mercedes Benz 180 and 190. As you start to step into the Lark you're prepared for the close quarters and that vaguely cramped feeling common to all imports priced under $3000.

Suddenly, as you slide into the seat and shut the door, the car seems to grow like Alice in Wonderland did when she ate the magic cake. What started out to be a small car has suddenly turned into a roomy, standard-

Lark

is the car

for you

if... You've long waited for a compact yet full-sized true economy car.

if... You want an easy-to-handle, maneuverable car with both powerful performance and excellent economy ... Lark V-8

if... Standard sized U.S. cars are too big and the imports are too small and both are too expensive.

LARK

SPECIFICATIONS

ENGINE	V-8	6
Bore and stroke	3-9/16 in. x 3¼ in.	3 in. x 4 in.
Displacement	259 cu. in.	170 cu. in.
Compression ratio	8.8:1	8.3:1
Max. brake horsepower	NA	NA
Max. torque	NA	NA
DIMENSIONS		
Wheelbase	108.5 in.	
Overall length	175 in.	
Overall width	69 in.	
Overall height	57.5 in.	
TRANSMISSIONS	Flightomatic, overdrive, syncromesh	

In addition to its two-door sedan,
Lark line includes four-door, two-door
hardtop and roomy two-door wagon.

Luggage space is adequate, but not ample.
Reduced trunk room is only sacrifice
to overall length of 175 inches.

sized sedan with 59-inch-wide seats and room for my 6-foot 2-inch frame in the rear seat, even with the front seat adjusted as far back as it would go.

On the road the dual personality of the Lark continued to amaze and delight me. Parking and maneuvering the car at slow speeds you get the feeling of a perky, nimble, light-on-its-wheels import such as an Opel or Renault Dauphine. Point this same car for the open road and in a matter of seconds you're rolling along at 70 with the solid control and cushiony ride of a full-sized and full-powered American car.

This combination of the best of both a roomy American car and a compact import comes as a brand new concept to the U.S. car market. It is a pretty near direct answer to the legion of critics who have been complaining loud and long that the standard U.S. passenger cars were "too big, too long and too clumsy".

The Lark is neither too long nor too big and it is certainly not clumsy. It seems to me to be the ideal package for the one-car family who wants more than a Volkswagen and less than a 210-inch-long-by-80-inch-wide, 250-horsepower 4000-lb. high-speed touring car.

Then too, the Lark offers the lowest-priced full-sized six passenger sedan available in the U.S. in the form of its DeLuxe six-cylinder two-door, which delivers at South Bend for approximately $1800, including Federal Excise Tax.

I hasten to add for the benefit of those who are familiar with the 1957-58 Stude Scotsman, that the Lark DeLuxe is not a "stripped" model. It comes with foam rubber cushions, rear windows that can be lowered, vinyl upholstery in place of cardboard, as well as front arm rests, sun visors, and just the right amount of chrome trim. For an additional $50 or so you can have the Lark DeLuxe as a four-door sedan. Studebaker's three-speed and torque converter automatic transmission, or synchromesh plus overdrive, are options on all models.

In addition to the sedans, the Lark line offers a two-door station wagon and a very sleek and smart two-door hardtop. The station wagon, incidentally, is on a chassis with five inches more wheelbase and is four inches longer overall, but still is only an inch longer than the Rambler American.

This Lark wagon is another amazing tribute to the ingenuity of Studebaker's resourceful engineering staff. In spite of the two foot reduction in overall length the wagon body is exactly the same size as on last year's Studebakers and Packards! What's more, it is available with an optional rearward facing third seat, which means that you can carry a full wagon-load of eight passengers. (With the third seat installed the wagon dispenses with the spare and comes equipped with "captive air" tires.)

To round out the versatility of this new line, all models except the two-door sedan can be bought with Studebaker's compact and smooth-running 259-cu. in. V-8. (Conversely, the two-door hardtop is available with V-8 only.)

Driving a Lark V-8 is an even more

STUDEBAKER LARK CHECK LIST ☑ ☑ ☑ ☑ ☑ 5 CHECKS MEAN TOP RATING IN ITS PRICE CLASS

Despite short outside dimensions, Lark passenger space is just the same as full-sized '58 Studebaker.

Studebaker's compact V-8 engine is available on all Lark models except regular two-door sedans.

amazing experience than piloting one of the perky sixes. Here again you start out with the psychological twist of approaching a small car and getting into a big one, driving about town with the light feeling of an import almost as maneuverable as a Volkswagen. But in this one you have five times the VW's 36 horsepower! The Lark V-8 takes off like a steam catapult and will get you to 60 mph in just 10.5 seconds. This acceleration potential is shaded by only the big, premium-priced V-8s.

The V-8-equipped models will delight those who have been dreaming of having a compact, maneuverable car in traffic plus more-than-ample power to perform out on the highway with the best of them.

SUMMING UP: In the Lark, Studebaker has come up with a really remarkable car — one that combines some of the best features of both large and small cars with few of the faults of either. It is the kind of car that many Americans really need — they have only to try it to find that out. ●

Category	Description	Rating
PERFORMANCE	Lark V-8 leads cars of its price and size in acceleration and high speed performance. The six-cylinder engine gives entirely adequate performance for a family car, is particularly suited to overdrive.	✔ ✔ ✔ ✔ ✔
STYLING	Studebaker has come up with a crisp well-balanced style treatment of a tough problem: how to make a short wide body look long and low. It adds up to an attractive and distinctive car.	✔ ✔ ✔ ✔
RIDING COMFORT	Both Lark Six and V-8 are comfortable-riding cars, on a par with their longer, heavier competition and far more comfortable than any import under $3000.	✔ ✔ ✔ ✔
INTERIOR DESIGN	Considering the room, accessibility, vision and comfort Studebaker has built into such compact dimensions, the Lark outshines them all.	✔ ✔ ✔ ✔ ✔
ROADABILITY	The Larks strike a nice average of all American cars and rate considerably above most imports. The V-8's roadability, better than the six's is very good indeed.	✔ ✔ ✔
EASE OF CONTROL	Here again the eight is above the average, with very good light and precise steering control, while the six feels a bit vague on winding roads because of its lightness and dual-ratio gear.	✔ ✔ ✔ ✔
ECONOMY	The Lark six will just about match its direct U.S. competition, which is very good indeed. The V-8 offers the greatest combination of performance and economy on the American road.	✔ ✔ ✔ ✔ ✔
SERVICEABILITY	The simple six has the edge here, but both cars are well above the U.S. average in engine compartment accessibility.	✔ ✔ ✔ ✔
WORKMANSHIP	Judging from pilot production cars, all Larks are going to be well above the average, especially in fit of trim and sheet metal panels.	✔ ✔ ✔ ✔
VALUE PER DOLLAR	Since the Lark is a brand new car, there is no depreciation pattern to compare with other makes. However, we'll predict that its depreciation will be favorable. As a straight purchase it is an excellent buy.	✔ ✔ ✔ ✔

STUDEBAKER LARK OVERALL RATING... 4.2 CHECKS

A LESS INSOLENT CHARIOT

Studebaker has responded hastily and well to a current author's plea

THE IRASCIBLE John Keats, whose title we have cribbed ("The Insolent Chariots," reviewed on page 60), would doubtless feel that we are pussyfooting here. He would probably disagree with our conclusions, too. Nonetheless, it appears to us that the past 10 years have been more significant than the demise of the Model T, which so traumatized him. Since the war, there has been a rapid movement away from the fundamental purpose of the automobile into a morass of status symbolism. Here appearance takes precedence over engineering; size, and sometimes the nameplate, are the criteria by which a car's worth is judged.

Yet there are many Americans who do not yearn for, and almost as many who actively do not want, a heavy, wide and astoundingly powered car. For sundry reasons, they have not bought imported cars: the true economy models seem cramped to them, the middle-sized sedans are generally expensive, and service seems or is a problem in their communities. A great many of them have bought Ramblers.

Studebaker, after several years of trying to compete with the big companies, has decided to excuse itself from a losing game and offer the conservative buyer something new. The better to concentrate, only the Lark, shown here, and a virtually unchanged Silver Hawk will be built. Both models are to be available with either the 6 or the V-8 engine.

The Lark should not be dismissed lightly by anyone, personally interested or not. There is absolutely no feeling at any time of driving or riding in a small, light car. The ride is extremely comfortable, yet, for an American car, it does not feel soft or mushy. It also rides quite flat, and high-speed stability seems excellent, although we were unable to try it in a cross-wind. The V-8 version of the Lark carries 57% of its curb weight on the front wheels, but we also drove it with four adults aboard, which changes the loading to 51/49. As a consequence the usually strong understeer (with driver only) becomes only moderate when the car is fully loaded. Minor changes in Studebaker's variable rate coil springs plus an effective anti-roll bar have resulted in very moderate roll angles, even with the driver alone and at high speeds on the skid pad.

The V-8, with automatic transmission, goes from 0 to 60 in about 12 seconds, and this was the 180–brake horsepower model. Studebaker engineers tell us that the 195-bhp version (four-barrel carburetor, dual exhausts) with stick shift will reduce this time to just under 10 seconds, and we believe it. Circling the 3-mile oval at South Bend, we approached a speedometer reading of 100 miles per hour several times without really trying. Certainly the V-8 version is a terrifically performing machine, but the 90-bhp 6 has more appeal to most buyers.

Impressions of the side-valve 6 must be based on driving the Hawk. This engine is a much improved derivation of the pre-war Champion unit. It may be recalled that more recent models of Studebaker's 6 had a stroke of 4.375 inches. For 1959, the stroke has gone back to 4.00 in., as used in 1941 and 1942. However, the later-type crank with larger main bearings and more counterweighting is used. This and various minor but important structural changes in the engine have eliminated our biggest objection to it: a certain amount of roughness under full-throttle acceleration. The new engine is smooth and quiet at all speeds and loads. In the heavier Hawk, acceleration is not so good as in the V-8 Lark, but it is still certainly adequate.

Criticisms of the Lark should perhaps include a somewhat sports car–biased opinion that the seats are a little too high and too close to the steering wheel. The transmission is obtrusive in front, but the rear floor is almost flat.

The instrumentation is commendably readable and the quality level of the interior is surprisingly high, considering the price. The car feels, and is, solidly built, without shakes or rattles, even on the well used prototype which we drove.

The Lark's weight is a surprise, but a partial contribution to its solid feel. The 6-cylinder version weighs 2783 pounds and the V-8 3143 (both with overdrive). Considering this, the economical-to-replace tire sizes may not be such a good idea: 5.90-15 is standard on the 6's, 6.40-15 optional on the 6's and standard on the V-8's and both wagons, 6.70-15 optional on the latter models.

A heavier stick shift transmission has prudently been provided on the V-8's. The standard version has 260 pounds-feet of torque at 2800 revolutions per minute, the "power kit" version 265 at 3100 rpm.

In summing up the Lark, we would say that the one word best describing the car is "honest"—an honest car for sensible, practical people who don't like insolence.

PHOTOGRAPHY:
JOSEPH H. WHERRY

Once again we have interior hood latches. In the Lark, they unveil either this 180-horsepower V-8 or the familiar side-valve 6. The V-8 (8.8:1 compression ratio, 259.2 cubic inches) is optional in the hardtop and sedan shown here, and in a two-door wagon. An especially low-priced two-door sedan comes only with the 90-horsepower 6, whose displacement has been reduced (!) to 169.6 cubic inches. The other bodies can be ordered with the cheaper 6-cylinder engine, now considerably smoother.

The new Lark sedan, although its wheelbase is only 108.5 inches, avoids the grim look of its bigger predecessor, the Scotsman. Recognizable Studebaker lines show up in the side views more than from the front or rear. A useful centered glove compartment and top and bottom padding distinguish the dash, and the speedometer is round! That old friend, the Hill Holder, is optional with stick shift, and there is a new reclining seat, as in the competing Rambler.

South Bend's designers and engineers have turned into automotive magicians.

'59 STUDEBAKER LARK

BIGGEST 'LITTLE' CAR

The Lark's handling is impressive for a car of its size. This is especially true of the V-8 model.

Front and rear of Stude Lark
are among cleanest in industry.
Bumpers are interchangeable.

BY AL BERGER

N THE WORLD

LET'S start right off by saying that the SPEED AGE staff is tremendously impressed by Studebaker's Lark line for 1959. This is, in our opinion, the small car the American market has been waiting for.

Shorter than its only U.S. rival, the Rambler American—it's only 14 inches longer than a Volkswagen—the Lark is the only small car from either side of the water to offer genuine, comfortable seating for six adults. Better still, it offers an excellent ride, good handling and performance superior to anything in its size and price range.

Seeing the car for the first time, the viewer's natural reaction is "Man, this is neat!" And "neat" is probably the one word that best describes the Lark. Small (it's three inches shorter than the American) and clean-lined (there's only one chrome rub-rail, which runs all the way round the car), the Lark really fits perfectly into the "compact car" category.

By fitting a 175-inch-long body on a 108½-inch wheelbase (compared, for example, with the 178-inch-long, 100-inch-wheelbase American), the Stude-

baker designers made it possible to place the seats between the axles, taking advantage of the full width of the car. Result: almost as much interior space as a Ford, Chevrolet or Plymouth—in a car three feet shorter.

This is probably the most striking feature of the Lark—it seems to be much bigger inside than out. It's as though the Studebaker designers had somehow taken a full-sized American car and magically placed it inside a small European car. In appearance, in parking maneuverability, and in economy, it's a small car. In seating and luggage space, in speed, pickup and soft, comfortable ride, it's a big car.

Under the hood you can have either Studebaker's new 170-cu. in. six or the 259-cu. in. V-8. The six is a new version of last year's 185-cu. in. engine. It has been destroked from 4⅜ inches to four (the bore remains three inches). But a redesigned combustion chamber—compression ratio has been raised from 7.5:1 to 8.3:1—new pistons and a new crankshaft with greater journal overlap have kept the horse-

SPECIFICATIONS:

SIX & EIGHT

ENGINE AND CHASSIS

CYLINDERS	SIX
	EIGHT
ARRANGEMENT	IN-LINE
	V
BORE	4 INCHES
	3.56 INCHES
STROKE	3 INCHES
	3.25 INCHES
DISPLACEMENT	169.5 CU. IN.
	259.2 CU. IN.
COMPRESSION RATIO	8.3:1
	8.8:1
MAXIMUM BHP	90 @ 4000 RPM
	180 @ 4500 RPM
VALVES	L-HEAD
	OHV
CARBURETION	1-BARREL
	2-BARREL
TRANSMISSION	3-SPEED MANUAL & OD
	AUTOMATIC
TURNING DIAMETER	40 FT. ⅝ IN.
	40 FT. ⅝ IN.
STEERING	WORM & SECTOR
	WORM & ROLLER
STEERING WHEEL TURNS	5½
	4½
TIRE SIZE	5.90 x 15
	6.40 x 15
BRAKE LINING AREA	147.4 SQ. IN.
	147.4 SQ. IN.
SUSPENSION: FRONT	VARIABLE-RATIO COIL
REAR	**LEAF**
WEIGHT (CURB)	2674
	2732
FUEL TANK CAPACITY	18 GALS.
	18 GALS.

DIMENSIONS

WHEELBASE	108.5 INCHES
TREAD: FRONT	57 3/8 INCHES
REAR	56 9/16 INCHES
OVERALL LENGTH	179 INCHES
OVERALL WIDTH	69 INCHES
OVERALL HEIGHT	57.5 INCHES
GROUND CLEARANCE	7 15/16 INCHES

PERFORMANCE

ACCELERATION THROUGH GEARS

0-30 MPH	5.3 SECONDS
	4.0 SECONDS
0-40 MPH	8.1 SECONDS
	5.4 SECONDS
0-50 MPH	11.5 SECONDS
	7.8 SECONDS
0-60 MPH	18.9 SECONDS
	9.9 SECONDS
MAXIMUM SPEED (IND)	89 MPH
	104 MPH
MAXIMUM TORQUE (LBS./FT. @ RPM)	145 @ 2000
	260 @ 2800
HP PER CU. IN.	.53
	.69
LBS. PER HP	29.7
	15.15

For an "economy" car, the Lark with V-8 is a very hot package.

Lark's dash is clean and functional. Glove compartment is in center under radio, speaker is on right. Padding on dash is an optional extra. Ash tray and lighter are long stretch from driver's seat.

power up.

The V-8 is the Silver Hawk engine. (The Silver Hawk, by the way, is still available for 1959; the Golden Hawk, along with its supercharged 289-cu. in. engine, has been discontinued.) With bore and stroke unchanged, displacement remains 259 cu. in. This engine, too, has a reworked combustion chamber, raising compression ratio from 8.3:1 to 8.8:1. The intake manifold has been redesigned, too, and a more efficient carburetor has been fitted. Studebaker engineers claim the new setup should deliver up to 15% better performance and 25% better economy than last year's version.

Three transmissions are available: a standard three-speed stick shift, three-speed manual with overdrive, and a Borg-Warner automatic transmission (three-speed torque converter type). All transmission options are available with either engine.

Now let's climb aboard. After you get over the "Good gosh, is this the same car I was just standing outside of?" reaction, the first thing a driver notices is that Studebaker has abandoned its "Cyclops Eye" speedometer for a good, old-fashioned round speedometer-odometer dial with clear, easy-to-read numbers. Water temperature and fuel gauges are in a matching dial alongside. As in most other modern cars, unfortunately, there are only colored lights to warn of low oil pressure or a discharging battery. The two dials are mounted in an oblong housing which is duplicated by the radio grille over on the right-hand side of the dash. The glove compartment is intelligently located in the center, where the driver can reach it without straining.

The full-width seats easily accommodate three passengers in front and three in the rear. We tried it with three six-foot men, and found plenty of leg and elbow room—even in the back seat with the front seat slid all the way back.

The one sacrifice for all this room in a 175-inch car is a certain amount of luggage space. The trunk is seven or eight inches shorter than on the 1958 models. But it runs the full width of the car, and will easily hold a normal family's luggage—at that, it's bigger than most trunks were a few years ago. At this point we turn the key-starter and take her out on the road. The "minimum" car, the six-cylinder two-door, with manual transmission, was a refreshing surprise. There was no feel-

Interior shot shows Lark to be a genuine six-placer despite compact overall length.

Trunk space is quite adequate even though Lark has a minimum of rear overhang. Spare tire is recessed into trunk flooring.

Six-cylinder engine, top left, is standard equipment, achieves 90 hp. V-8 mill, left, optional on all models except the two-door sedan, can put forth a very healthy 180 hp with dual carbs.

ing of lack of power—the car had all the dig required for normal driving. Our 0-60 time of 18.9 seconds is not to be compared to the big-inch jobs, but it will match anything in the Lark's size and price class except the Volvo —which is only a four-passenger car. Allowing for the fact that our Lark was a long way from broken in and was carrying three big men, that's pretty good.

The ride was excellent—Studebaker has modified its variable-ratio coil springs so that they ride softer on the small bumps and get firmer on the big jounces, so that it is just about impossible to make them bottom. There is very little body shake and no rattles or vibration—the engineering department found that they had saved so much weight by shortening the frame that they could use heavier gauge

stock for greater rigidity.

The six handles well enough, but the variable-ratio worm-and-sector steering is not as good as, say, Ford's recirculating ball type or the rack-and-pinion version on some of the imports. But the car steers easily—we felt no need for power steering in parking. Roll and pitch were negligible, and there was little or no tire squeal.

Then we switched to a V-8, the two-door hardtop with overdrive. This one is in a different performance class entirely. It really digs out—we reached 60 in 10.5 seconds. And the speed-ometer hit 105 at one point on the straightaway. Handling was considerably better than on the six—the V-8 is equipped with a more efficient steering box with roller-bearing studs, and it shows on the tight turns. The body felt commendably solid for a hardtop,

with very little shake and no rattle—and the prototype we were driving did *not* have the beefed-up frame that will be on the production models.

A four-door sedan with the V-8 and automatic transmission came next. This one is a very nearly ideal family transportation package. The automatic transmission is the tried-and-true Borg-Warner three-speed torque converter used on a number of American and British cars, and it is as smooth as silk. We got our best acceleration with this model, by a slight margin, reaching 60 mph in exactly 9.9 seconds. This I defy any remotely comparable car to match!

In short, we liked the Lark. As one of our colleagues said as we left the Studebaker proving grounds, "If the American public doesn't go for this one, they'll *deserve* Volkswagens." ●

wheels
NEW CAR TRYOUT

The Studebaker Lark is a small car by gigantic American standards, compares in dimension with Australia's Holden. Performance and road holding are most impressive, according to tester Lyell.

Oh.

TAKE one Holden. From under the bonnet remove the six-cylinder, 70 horsepower motor, and replace it with a big, hairy 180 horsepower V8 unit, and for all practical purposes you've got yourself a 1959 Studebaker Lark four-door sedan.

The two car bodies are not really as easily interchangeable as this, but the comparison is valid, because for one thing the new Lark VIII is 1 in. shorter than Australia's Own, with roughly the same equipment, seating capacity, interior dimensions and, finish.

But when it comes to engine-room equipment the Lark parts company with the Holden — a dry weight of 26½ cwt. gives it a power/ratio weight of 134 b.h.p. per ton. Put that in your scrapbook of impressive mechanical feats!

If you're frightened by the vision of possessing all this power under your hoof, with not even a gear-shift to twiddle with in the idle moments between 100-mile posts, don't be.

Once you have escaped the feeling that with brutal acceleration you might permanently dislocate your neck, it is exhilarating. But more later about this encounter with the rocket age.

The Lark VIII, you'll recall, is

Driver sits behind slightly dished steering wheel and has full view of instruments on the simply arranged dashboard. Auto transmission selector is on right side of the steering column.

As small as a Holden, but with more than twice as much power, Studebaker's Lark is ball of fire, discovers WHEEL's tester PETER LYELL.

what a Lark!

Studebaker's big bid to muscle in on the small car market in America, pioneered three years ago with considerable courage by Rambler. The Lark is designed to invade this hard-won Rambler field, and to compete with the increasingly popular European cars biting chunks out of American local car sales.

The front of the Lark—the most unusual and distinguishing feature of its styling—shows disrespect for popular U.S. design cliches, such as dual headlights and broad, complex radiator grilles. At rear, believe it or not, there's nothing that might be described as a fin. The resulting appearance of the car as a whole is pleasantly uncluttered and almost brutally simple. But it grows on you — because it's so obviously a functionally designed carriage.

Three examples of the Lark VIII have been imported into Australia —four-door sedans, two-door hardtops and two-door station waggons. All three are fitted with V8 motors with a single twin-throat carburettor. In this form the 4.4-litre unit develops 180 b.h.p. at 4,500 r.p.m., and a torque of 260 ft./lbs. at 2,800 r.p.m. on compression ratio of 8.3 to 1. Bore is 3.56 in., stroke 3.25 in. —well "oversquare".

All three models are fitted with Flightomatic automatic transmission, controlled by a steering column selector lever with indicator segment.

The V8 has been packed under the Lark's frank, sawn-off bonnet with amazingly little room to spare. With a large hat-type air cleaner, a 12-volt battery mounted high up on the nearside, a heater and a windscreen washer water bag occupying the four corners around the motor, there's little room to fiddle with any of the works.

The Lark's stylists, it seems, were quite rightly more concerned about the comfort of passengers than the

Packed tight into the dumpy engine compartment, the Lark's V/8 does not look as impressive as the road performance feels.

convenience of mechanics, because at the other end there's a deep boot big enough to hold four or five small boys, and in between, a spacious compartment for six people.

The boot, incidentally, is of the high-walled type, out of which you *lift* heavy objects rather than *drag* them out—a trap which the Lark designers fell into deliberately, in the interests of rear end styling.

Inside, the Lark is austere by American standards, but completely adequate, right down to the instruments discreetly embedded in the facia.

There are two simple dials: a speedometer calibrated to an alarm-

ing 120 m.p.h. — which, with that husky V8 under the bonnet, you take very seriously — and another showing fuel and engine temperature. These are both beautifully visible through the dished, two-spoke steering wheel with horn ring on the lower half.

Four pull-knobs and a starter-ignition lock complete the instrumentation. A pull-and-twist handbrake (when will designers see the futility of using these contraptions?) is located under the panel close to the steering column.

CONTINUED ON PAGE 68

For those who would consider seating space with their sport . . . take a look at the <u>supercharged</u>

Studebaker Golden Hawk

Finned drums provide efficient air cooling of brakes.

Non-slip differential sends power to rear wheel with the best traction, not poorest.

Two-stage blower delivers boost when needed, idles at cruise speeds.

Instrumentation is functional, attractive. Switches are toggle for efficient use.

Very few cars produced anywhere in the world—having an honest 5 or 6-passenger seating capacity—offer the performance and handling qualities you can enjoy in a Golden Hawk. A 289 cu. in. engine teamed with a two-stage, built-in supercharger, gives the car a weight-to-power ratio of approximately 12:1. The resulting performance is complemented by large, finned brake drums that efficiently minimize fade. The brakes are self-centering and self-energizing.

A very desirable sports car characteristic of the Golden Hawk is its slight degree of understeer. A knowledgeable driver can slide a Hawk through a corner and hold the car on its line or correct with throttle and a flick of the wrists. For optimum use of power at the rear wheels, a non-slip differential* is available. To augment driving efficiency, the Hawk has complete, functional instrumentation which includes a tachometer and manifold pressure gauge.

Why not test-drive a Golden Hawk and form your own conclusions? And remember, the Golden Hawk means fun for the *entire family.*

*Studebaker-Packard Twin Traction differential.

 Studebaker-Packard

CORPORATION

Where pride of Workmanship comes first!

road test

STUDEBAKER LARK

A new and better product in last year's wrappings

I T IS NO secret that last year's Lark 6 failed to come up to expectations in some departments, particularly fuel consumption. In fact, the V-8 engine option would, under most driving conditions, get better mileage than the 6. In our road test of the 6, which appeared in March 1959, we reported 17/22 mpg and this figure was corroborated by other magazines and by Bill Corey's preliminary Mobilgas test runs. We also reported "performance which may be adequate, but can hardly be called sparkling" and "considerable air intake noise at high revs."

With a year's production experience and several small but significant mechanical changes for 1960, the Lark 6 is now virtually a completely different automobile. The difference is so great that a little explanation may be in order. The mechanical changes include a revised combustion chamber for better engine smoothness, an entirely new carburetor, new engine mounts and, most important to acceleration performance, revised axle ratios. Anyone stepping out of a '59 and into a '60 will immediately note the tremendous improvement in smoothness and silence.

Performance, too, is now up to where it should be. Our test car for this report was a fully equipped two-door hardtop and it weighed 150 lb more than last year's standard two-door sedan. However, the 1960 car was also equipped with overdrive and the accompanying change in axle ratio more than compensated for the added weight. The comparative data show the difference in performance better than words:

	1959	1960
Curb weight	2750	2900
Test weight	3040	3200
Axle ratio	3.54	4.10
Time, 0-60	21.0	17.9
High gear pull, lb-ton	185	200
Mpg	17/22	19/25

The fuel consumption figures need a little further ex-

planation because of the overdrive. We found the overdrive not too useful and we rate the new Lark as being 2 to 3 mpg better than last year without using the overdrive and despite the added weight and 4.10 axle. In other words, the lighter two-door sedan, without overdrive (3.73 axle), should return even better economy than is recorded here.

As for the overdrive's usefulness, the overall ratio provided (2.87) is absurdly high as shown by the Volkswagen-like Tapley pull reading of only 135 lb/ton. Such

In the era of the dollar grin, a refreshingly simple approach.

Vinyl-covered cowl reflects interior improvements.

PHOTOS BY POOLE

The old Champion enters the compact ring.

a ratio is useful on long, level stretches of road, when cruising at 60 to 70 mph, but a strong headwind will actually slow the car and passing reserve is virtually nil. In addition, the Lark is definitely faster in direct drive; 82 honest mph in high gear is equivalent to 4430 rpm, not too far past the peak power point. The same speed is impossible to reach in overdrive, except downhill, but would be equivalent to only 3100 rpm, at which point the maximum engine power is no more than 70 bhp—not enough (70 bhp, in a car of this size and weight, and with optimum axle ratio, would give a true top speed of no more than 78 mph). Accordingly, the calculated data given in the panel are all based on high gear, or direct drive.

The theoretical cruising speed given for overdrive (99.1 mph) is, of course, not attainable under any circumstances. An incidental advantage of the overdrive is that it can be used to give an extra ratio: 2nd-overdrive. The overall ratio in that gear is 4.676 (0.70 x 1.63 x 4.10). This ratio gives acceleration, pulling power and

grade ability about 14% better than high gear, and can be very useful, especially on mountain roads, because there is no free-wheeling above 30 mph and a modest 4000 rpm is still a good rate of knots—65 mph, to be exact. For those interested, the comparison is as follows:

	High Gear	Over-drive	1959 Test
Effective axle ratio	4.10	2.87	3.54
Lb/hp (test wt)	35.6	35.6	33.8
Cu ft/ton mile	99.2	69.3	90.2
Mph/1000 rpm	18.5	26.5	21.4
Engine revs/mile	3240	2270	2795
Piston travel, ft/mile	2160	1510	1860
Rpm @ 2500 ft/min	3750	3750	3750
equivalent mph	69.5	99.1	80.5
R&T wear index	70.0	34.3	52.0

In general, the rest of the car is pretty much like last year's report. One important exception is that the quality

You'll have to look inside to find the 1960 changes.

King-size room for a compact package.

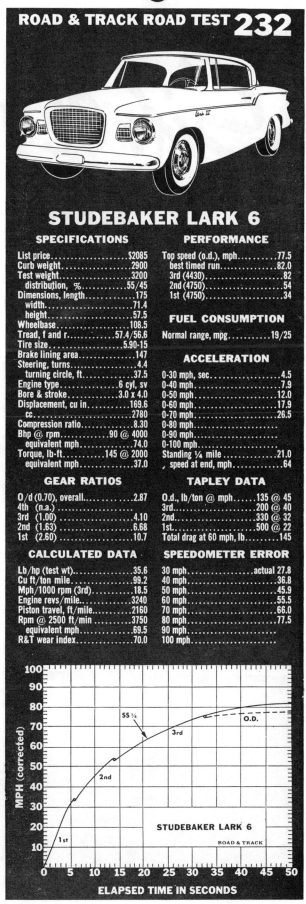

ROAD & TRACK ROAD TEST 232

STUDEBAKER LARK 6

SPECIFICATIONS		PERFORMANCE	
List price	$2085	Top speed (o.d.), mph	77.5
Curb weight	2900	best timed run	82.0
Test weight	3200	3rd (4430)	82
distribution, %	55/45	2nd (4750)	54
Dimensions, length	175	1st (4750)	34
width	71.4		
height	57.5	**FUEL CONSUMPTION**	
Wheelbase	108.5		
Tread, f and r	57.4/56.6	Normal range, mpg	19/25
Tire size	5.90-15		
Brake lining area	147	**ACCELERATION**	
Steering, turns	4.4		
turning circle, ft	37.5	0-30 mph, sec	4.5
Engine type	6 cyl, sv	0-40 mph	7.9
Bore & stroke	3.0 x 4.0	0-50 mph	12.0
Displacement, cu in	169.6	0-60 mph	17.9
cc	2780	0-70 mph	26.5
Compression ratio	8.30	0-80 mph	
Bhp @ rpm	90 @ 4000	0-90 mph	
equivalent mph	74.0	0-100 mph	
Torque, lb-ft	145 @ 2000	Standing ¼ mile	21.0
equivalent mph	37.0	speed at end, mph	64

GEAR RATIOS		TAPLEY DATA	
O/d (0.70), overall	2.87	O.d., lb/ton @ mph	135 @ 45
4th (n.a.)		3rd	200 @ 40
3rd (1.00)	4.10	2nd	330 @ 32
2nd (1.63)	6.68	1st	500 @ 22
1st (2.60)	10.7	Total drag at 60 mph, lb	145

CALCULATED DATA		SPEEDOMETER ERROR	
Lb/hp (test wt)	35.6	30 mph	actual 27.8
Cu ft/ton mile	99.2	40 mph	36.8
Mph/1000 rpm (3rd)	18.5	50 mph	45.9
Engine revs/mile	3240	60 mph	55.5
Piston travel, ft/mile	2160	70 mph	66.0
Rpm @ 2500 ft/min	3750	80 mph	77.5
equivalent mph	69.5	90 mph	
R&T wear index	70.0	100 mph	

level appears to be much improved. Such items as door fit and trim detail show better workmanship and improved quality control. In addition, the Regal hardtop body style has a much more impressive interior treatment than does the rather plain two-door sedan. The entire dash and cowl are covered in a leather-like material (vinyl) which looks very good. Two new de luxe options that look especially interesting are adjustable reclining seats and headrests—both ideas are right out of Stuttgart. Options like an automatic transmission and power assists are available on the 6, but we can't see why anyone would want them in a car such as this, which is designed and intended to be sensible, economical transportation, and succeeds very well at it.

One item not carried over from last year was a very accurate speedometer. This test car had considerable error, though the percentage of optimism did become less at higher speeds. Last year's car had a speedometer that was actually slow at 70 and 80 mph.

As before, the ride is very good by American car standards, though rather too soft by ours. In other words, anyone used to a large U.S. car will not feel any depreciation in riding qualities and will like the easier, lighter handling of the compact car. The car is very stable at high speeds but could use stiffer dampers to advantage over wallowing-type roads. The turning circle (37.5 ft) is surprisingly large for this size car, but the short overhangs at each end make it very easy to park. In this connection, the V-8 engine option, which adds 320 lb to the weight (and most of that in front), isn't too good and power steering may be advisable as a slight penalty for those who want dazzling V-8 performance in a compact sedan.

In comparison with the other 20-odd compacts now on the market, the Lark 6 has certain special advantages. Probably the most important of these is the fact that the Lark provides the easiest entrance and exit, with nearly flat floors (at least there is no step-down), chair-height seats and a roof edge high enough to lessen the danger of rapping one's head. A second special advantage of the Lark is undoubtedly its practical design from the standpoint of simplicity and servicing ease.

Finally, the Lark 6 is a design of proven durability. The 6-cyl engine, for example, is the old Champion, with many worthwhile improvements. Studebaker likes to point out that the Lark is "a highly refined and subtly improved automobile, proven by 750 million miles of owner use." We have nothing more to add—we agree.

Silver Hawk:

Detroit's untarnished

Studebaker's glamorous Silver Hawk is a rare cross between Continental styling and Detroit tradition. Nevertheless, reports DOUG BLAIN, this is a desirable tool.

Coined dashboard is actually a casting and not the real thing, but instrumentss are impressively simple. Tryout car had efficient auto transmission. Box under scuttle is heater.

Cornered hard the Silver Hawk leans, but not excessively. Handling and brakes have distinct American flavour.

FOR years Studebaker's Hawk series has intrigued us. We think perhaps the Hawks intrigue most people.

Are they really sports cars? Do those delightful, Continental lines cover just another sloppy old Detroiter or is there individuality deep down inside as well?

A brief encounter with the latest import in the line, the 1959 Silver Hawk, answered most of our questions and a few more besides.

Let's start with appearance. The Silver Hawk is a simplified version of its Golden cousin. The one we tried was red, with a pleasant lack of chromium embellishment. True, it had fins and wrap-arounds and most of the other external whatnots that so many people criticise in U.S. cars, but they were subtly blended into a shapely whole. We spoke to no one who wasn't suitably impressed.

Power comes from a big 4248 c.c. V8 on an 8.8 to 1 compression. Bore/stroke ratio is well oversquare at 90.4 by 82.5 mm. Maximum power is a reasonable 180 developed at 4,500 r.p.m.

The engine does not have the Golden Hawk's supercharger—a simplified device which used to pressurise cold air before feeding it to the carburettor.

The Silver Hawk has two doors, both of them wide enough to make entry to a full-size (well, almost) back seat easy even for the aged and the elongated.

The front seat is an unsporting bench, slightly more sensibly shaped than most. Headroom in front is generous in spite of the car's small overall height. In the back things aren't quite so bright. Leg-room there is just adequate.

Cotton link carpet covers the floor. The dashboard is quietly

wheels
NEW CAR TRYOUT

emblem of nicety

Sure, it has got tail fins, but we'll get you won't find nicer looking ones in all America. The Silver Hawk seats four to five people and under that bonnet is a great big hairy V/8 engine.

trimmed in simulated coined aluminium. The glovebox lid on our tryout car had fallen inwards and refused to open. Instruments are well lettered in white on round black dials with simple chromium bezels. The Silver Hawk has a huge clock opposite the speedometer instead of a tachometer. Ours had a cigarette lighter, but it was stuck in the "on" position and had to be left out.

The driving position is good, with the reservation that backward seat adjustment has to be limited out of consideration for rear passengers. The wheel is set high, rather destroying any sports car pretensions. Our Hawk had automatic transmission, once again giving the lie to those rakish lines.

You get the impression as the engine fires that the car is going to prove a real performer. It burbles like a thoroughbred through its twin exhausts and engine noise even at the driver's seat is considerable.

You sit back, select Drive on the column sector and push gingerly on the big organ throttle pedal Noth-

ing happens. You think again and push harder. With a lurch that is the penalty for strong pedal return springs (mustn't frighten granny, Mr. Engineer — keep it high so she can't flatten her foot) the lusty V8 grumbles into life. For a split second the back wheels chirp and churn at the road surface. Then the limited-slip differential system gets the better of all that torque and the sleek American charges away, leaving you wondering what happened to the traffic back there as you feel for the brakes.

Yes, the Studebaker Silver Hawk does accelerate. It may not have the cubic inches of some of its garish cousins, but it is much, much lighter than they and the result is a power/weight ratio approaching the magical 200 b.h.p./ton.

Cornering is very good by American standards. The car doesn't lean excessively Its tyres don't even squeal beyond reasonable limits. Unfortunately low gearing (four and a half turns) and an objectionable lack of self-centring take the keen edge off the pleasure of driving the Hawk quickly.

Braking, too, is a little disappointing. Soft linings help to give good initial retardation, but a series of quick dabs at the pedal from fairly high speeds produced fade and a bad pull to the left during our drive.

Did we expect too much from the Silver Hawk? Possibly, although expect is not the word. We never expect anything when we drive a new car. We approached the Hawk purely with the object of matching up its delightful appearance with its promising mechanical specification.

The fact that one is Continental while the other remains distinctly American at heart will probably please many people. And after all, the Hawk costs much less than many of its competitors.

It should also be cheaper to run and in lots of ways more satisfying. Undoubtedly longer acquaintance would produce many more endearing features than we were able to find in two hours.

(Tryout car from Ira L. and A. C. Berk, Sydney. List price £2,801 including tax).   #

A Gran Turismo car for the sporting family

HAWK 4-SPEED

IN THE FALL OF 1952 we attended the announcement showing of a new car. It wasn't the usual press party, complete with public relations men and ready-made publicity handouts, but was, instead, the first showing to the dealers handling the line. The car was the 1953 Studebaker, designed by Raymond Loewy Associates, and the place was the Shrine Auditorium in Los Angeles. It was a special occasion—aside from introducing a completely new car—for it was the 100th anniversary of the Studebaker Corporation.

After a one-hour-long stage show the curtains were drawn on the closing act, the stage lights dimmed and when the curtains were re-opened to the accompaniment of a fanfare from the orchestra, the 6500 people in the audience got their first look at one of the best-looking production cars ever built, anywhere. After the "is it

coming or going" Studebakers of the post World War II era—so prized as a subject by comedians—culminating in the "airplane-nosed" model in 1952, merely to say that these dealers were ecstatic is the understatement of the year.

Since that model, only minor visible changes have been made in the car; most of the improvements have been detail refinements made continually over the last eight years. The 1953 chassis and main body shell are continued in the 1961 model almost unchanged. A new hood and deck lid were added in 1956 for the first of the Hawk series. In 1957, fins were added (without visual improvement, we might add); they were made of fiberglass and were installed right over the stock 1953–56 rear fenders.

The hood, deck and fins are still with us (or, more rightly, with the car) although the fins are now made of sheet steel. The first Hawks were the hardtop coupe version—formerly called the Starliner—while a less expensive version, designated the Starlight, used the same body shell but was what is commonly called a five-window coupe.

At first, either coupe was available as a V-8 or L-head six and with a Borg-Warner 3-speed automatic transmission, or a 3-speed column shift with or without overdrive. For 1961 the coupe is available only as a V-8 with the five-window coupe body, and transmission options consist of the familiar 3-speed automatic or 3-speed column shift with or without overdrive and, for the first time, a Warner Gear (Corvette) 4-speed, all synchromesh floorshift gearbox. This latter version is the subject of our test.

We've pretty well covered the appearance of the Hawk, other than to say that the finish, trim and panel fit of our test car were very good, inside and out.

Climbing into the driver's seat, which, like the passenger's seat, is a fully reclining, individual semi-bucket, one gets the impression of sitting inside a purposeful Grand Touring car. The feeling is further enhanced by the functional, round, white on black instruments set into an "engine turned" aluminum panel and the floor shift control knob which is perfectly positioned.

The clutch is smooth and the response from the willing engine is instantaneous, but pulling out of the driveway into traffic forcefully brings to mind the 120.5-in. wheelbase and 204-in. over-all length. Even though the car is responsive and easy to drive, it does take up a lot of space on the road.

Shifting up (or down) through the gears is done without effort and the smoothness of the transmission is very enjoyable. This unit is the same as the one installed in the Corvette, so it is not an unknown quantity, though new to the Hawk this year.

We missed a tachometer, though mostly just because we're used to driving with one—it is not really needed. This feeling also may have been partly due to the fine transmission, which invited constant use, and the pleasant gear whine accompanying the lower three gears, but the fact that a tach is missing was made more apparent by the unfilled space allotted for it in the panel. We feel that it should be included as standard equipment because the extra cost ($53.80) for this accessory is not high enough

to drive away very many of the potential Hawk buyers.

The afore-mentioned 204-in. length is not too noticeable when out on the open road, and it is here that the car is at its best. The lengthy wheelbase even has some value, as the tendency to pitch on undulating surfaces is very low and when pitch *does* occur, as it will on some surfaces, it is not as excessive as it might be in a car with a shorter wheelbase.

Visibility is good, but not excellent. The sloping hood and relatively narrow front fenders make forward vision very good, but the Hawk is still plagued with the thick windshield/door posts it has had since 1953.

Having owned one of the 1953 Loewy Studebaker coupes with a body style identical to that of our test car, we were able to notice many improvements in spite of the definite similarity to the older model. The seats in the 1961 version are more comfortable, due for the most part to the switch to individual seats in place of the bench-type in the earlier models. A little more leg room has been created for rear seat passengers by clever redesign of the rear seat itself. We had found, in several years of

CONTINUED

driving this model, that adults could make long trips in the rear seat if frequent stops were made for stretching, or, even better, for front and rear seat passengers to swap seats. Children up to, say, age 12 can ride in reasonable comfort (outside of their normal inclination to become restless and irritable in confined areas) for a considerable distance.

Obviously a coupe like the Studebaker cannot be as comfortable for rear seat passengers as a sedan would be, but this is supposed to be a Grand Touring car which, by assumed definition, should be sleek and have a sporting look—something that is virtually impossible in a functional sedan design.

Our test car had power steering and power brakes, neither of which we consider absolutely necessary. However, the power steering did come in handy in parking because of the front-heavy weight bias of the car. Because of the preponderance of weight on the front wheels, some front end "plowing" was experienced when curves were approached at too great a speed.

A few years ago we quickened the steering on a Champion (six) Studebaker coupe—after weighing it and an identical V-8, for fore and aft loading as well as total. The steering change was accomplished by relocating the hole in the steering bell-crank where the drag link connects to it, thus speeding up the steering by about 15%. This could be done quite satisfactorily on the Champ because its relatively light weight at the front end didn't make the steering appreciably heavier. It would have been impractical on the V-8, especially one with the heavy automatic transmission, unless the car had been equipped with power steering.

Trunk space was improved a little when the squared-off deck lid was adopted in 1956, but we still found the space somewhat awkward to use because the spare tire and gas filler pipe took up so much of the flat floor area. If the car is used as a GT car, rather than something that is supposed to replace the family station wagon, the luggage capacity is certainly adequate and quite a bit of "soft luggage" can be gotten into the trunk.

A buyer who is sports car oriented and has cut his teeth on an MG, Porsche or Alfa Romeo will probably be disappointed in the Hawk because it is softly sprung and very large compared to a sports car, but to the potential buyer who is accustomed to the size, performance and handling of most domestic cars, the Hawk will be a refreshing change. And, we emphatically state that the Hawk is a touring car (Grand), not a sports car or a family sedan.

A family man who covets a sports or GT car, but who can afford only one, would do well to examine the Hawk, because it does combine the sporting characteristics of the imports with the usable space and rugged dependability of the U.S. product. One word of caution—just don't try to follow a well driven Giulietta into a decreasing-radius turn too fast.

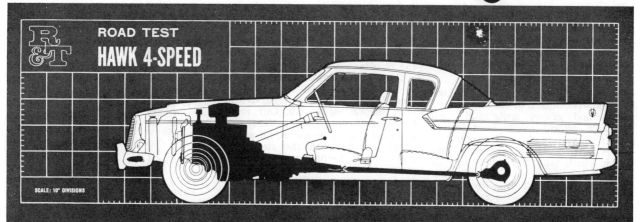

ROAD TEST
HAWK 4-SPEED

SCALE: 10" DIVISIONS

DIMENSIONS

Wheelbase, in	120.5
Tread, f and r	57.4/56.6
Over-all length, in	204
width	71.3
height	55.5
equivalent vol, cu ft	421
Frontal area, sq ft	19.9
Ground clearance, in	6.9
Steering ratio, o/a	27.5
turns, lock to lock	4.6
turning circle, ft	41
Hip room, front	59.5
Hip room, rear	58.0
Pedal to seat back	44.0
Floor to ground	12.0

CALCULATED DATA

Lb/hp (test wt)	17.6
Cu ft/ ton mile	114
Mph/1000 rpm (4th)	26.8
Engine revs/mile	2460
Piston travel, ft/mile	1483
Rpm @ 2500 ft/min	4120
equivalent mph	100.8
R&T wear index	36.5

SPECIFICATIONS

List price	$3415
Curb weight, lb	3350
Test weight	3710
distribution, %	57/43
Tire size	6.70–15
Brake lining area	172.8
Engine type	V-8, ohv
Bore & stroke	3.56 x 3.62
Displacement, cc	4738
cu in	289
Compression ratio	8.8
Bhp @ rpm	210 @ 4500
equivalent mph	110.0
Torque, lb-ft	300 @ 2800
equivalent mph	68.5

GEAR RATIOS

4th (1.0)		3.31
3rd (1.31)		4.34
2nd (1.66)		5.49
1st (2.20)		7.28

SPEEDOMETER ERROR

30 mph	actual, 28.5
60 mph	55.7

PERFORMANCE

Top speed (4700), mph	115
best timed run	n.a.
3rd (5000)	93
2nd (5050)	74
1st (5050)	56

FUEL CONSUMPTION

Normal range, mpg	14/18

ACCELERATION

0–30 mph, sec	3.8
0–40	5.2
0–50	7.1
0–60	10.2
0–70	14.0
0–80	19.5
0–100	
Standing ⅓ mile	17.3
speed at end	76.0

TAPLEY DATA

4th, lb/ton @ mph	280 @ 74
3rd	370 @ 62
2nd	475 @ 55
Total drag at 60 mph, lb	139

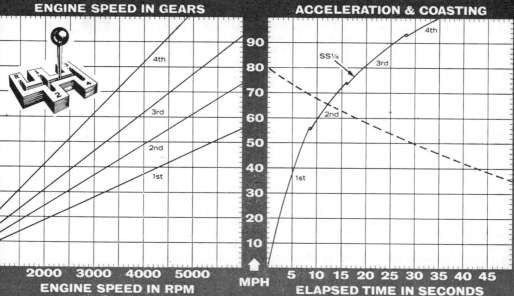

ENGINE SPEED IN GEARS

4th
3rd
2nd
1st

ENGINE SPEED IN RPM
2000 3000 4000 5000

ACCELERATION & COASTING

4th
SS¼
3rd
2nd
1st

MPH
ELAPSED TIME IN SECONDS
5 10 15 20 25 30 35 40 45

Studebaker's Golden Hawk

CONTINUED FROM PAGE 13
normal driving. We sailed at high speed over dozens of bad dips, holes, dirt and gravel spots and even though almost every imperfection in the road made itself known, it was a friendly acquaintance and one which tended to build up our confidence in the car. The steering felt perhaps a trifle slow for so fast a car, but dead accurate and free from play, and there was a slight but pleasant degree of understeer. When certain corners were taken with a bit too much enthusiasm the car forgave us, slowly and politely, sliding outwards across the road, never giving any suggestion of wanting to spin.

Already the acceleration of this automatic-transmission car (a standard shift and overdrive is available) was proving to be nothing short of amazing and the impossible-looking 30-per-cent grade was swallowed in one ferocious gulp, so quickly, in fact, that the Hawk nearly left the ground at the crest. A few more fast corners, with no side sway and not enough lean to make the passengers uncomfortable, and we found ourselves back in front of the high-speed track. Here is what we had been waiting for.

First we took a few fast laps around the three-mile track, banked at either end, to get the feel of the car "at speed." The faster we went the better it felt and that same understeer stood us in good stead as we hit the curves harder and harder. Soon we were coming off the longer of the two banked curves at an indicated 95 mph, and since this led into a completely-flat .8-mile stretch we decided to run our top-speed tests right then and there. Floorboarded at 95 mph (actually closer to an honest 90) the Golden Hawk fairly leaped ahead and we got nearly 115 before we had to back off for the turn ahead. This was tried several times and several runs of 115 mph and better were achieved with the car still accelerating. Then we just ran out of room. On the faster Packard track in Detroit, Bill Holland did nearly 125 mph with a Golden Hawk and this, we feel, is closer to its true top speed.

If you have been wondering, by the way, what the heavier Packard engine has done to the balance of the Studebaker, let us say that the car does seem noticeably heavier at the front than last year's Speedster, but this works out seemingly to its advantage.

With a fifth wheel and electric speedometer connected to the car,

we proceeded to run off our acceleration tests. We made half a dozen runs to each speed, in both directions, just to be sure, and here are the results:

Zero-to-30-mph time averaged out to 3.4 seconds. To 40 mph took 5.1 seconds and to 45 just eight-tenths of a second more—5.9. Our zero-to-60-mph runs hit an average of 9 seconds flat. These were all actual speeds, taken with the stopwatch and throttle being punched at the same instant, rather than waiting for the car to move. Using the latter method you could hit 60 mph in just a fraction over 8 seconds, but we'd rather be honest about it. Besides, these figures are pretty fantastic as they stand, even for an honest-to-goodness sports car. We tried several runs to 80 mph in the lower drive range of the Ultramatic transmission (the range used for all fast acceleration tests) and forgot at first that it keeps the car in third gear until you lift your foot for an instant. The result was that the engine peaked out at about 79 mph on our first try and we had to go back and do it again. This time the transmission was upshifted nicely and a run of 17.8 seconds was recorded from zero to 80 mph. This figure proved to be just about average.

All through our acceleration tests we had been checking the brakes as well. The Golden Hawk is equipped this year with new finned brakes that are designed to reduce fade. After every acceleration run, to every speed, we slammed the brakes on hard, and after more than 25 such applications they had definitely faded, requiring much greater pedal pressure. But at all times the car could be brought to a stop and one fast lap around the track was sufficient to bring them back almost to normal.

The only test that we didn't make with the Golden Hawk was one for gasoline mileage. Actually it should be quite economical considering the fact that the engine will be loafing most of the time at normal highway speeds. But we didn't feel that gas mileage was a strong consideration with a vehicle of this type, and so didn't take the time to run off our usual test.

With everything else considered, however, we nominate this as the American sports-type car of the year to beat. It's got everything from looks to handling to speed to plenty of room for four or five people. Every sort of power-assist equipment is available but we'll bet that lots of the Hawks will be sold with standard shift and regular steering. That's the way we'd like to own one. And the price is right, too. Suggested list in South Bend for the basic model of the Golden Hawk is $2,800. We would still call it a

lot of car for $1,000 more than that. If you really like to drive, be sure to take a close look at this one It's the end. ●

CONTINUED FROM PAGE 30
are 4in longer (and assembled with the rear axle forward of the centre line, to give added resistance to dip under braking and acceleration) are claimed to have improved the ride; an improved stabilizer bar complements the front suspension. A limited slip differential, a Studebaker-Packard feature, is still available.

Captive-Air tyres, claimed to eliminate the need for a spare, are provided on the Provincial and Scotsman station wagons when what is termed the Hideaway seat (optional) is fitted to increase passenger capacity from 6 to 8. This seat can be folded away to occupy the space normally taken by the spare wheel.

The President sedan and hardtop, the Golden Hawk and the vee-8 Silver Hawk have finned brake drums to improve their cooling and fade-resistance.

Flightomatic automatic transmission is available on all except the Scotsman station wagon and sedan, and overdrive is on option for all models having the standard three-speed transmission.

New trim materials with intriguing names decorate the interiors of the latest cars. For instance, the President Classic "combines fabric insert pleats of a Jacquard woven Abstract pattern of Ratine yarns, with finely textured, light-coloured nylon bolsters. On the padded door panels, Royal Moroccan grain vinyl accent panels contrast with a Shantung vinyl. Floor coverings are a matching, two-tone deep pile carpeting."

CAR LIFE ROAD TEST

STUDEBAKER LARK VI

As is well known, Studebaker builds two Lark models, a six and a V-8. For 1961 the 6-cylinder engine got a thorough redesign in order to boost its power and performance.

What isn't so well known is the fact that this redesigned six got its boost in power and performance with absolutely no sacrifice in fuel economy, no small feat in this day and age.

For this test report, *Car Life* tried two 6-cylinder Larks, both with stick shift. All the test data included here were taken on a showroom stock model, but just for kicks we also tried a factory test car set up for the Mobilgas Economy Run held in April. In the run an identical car averaged 26.67 mpg and our factory "practice" car had carburetor jets one size leaner, as permitted by the rules.

This practice car was equipped with extra instrumentation and in a special test we recorded 31.5 miles per gallon by feather-footing at 45 mph over a distance of about 4 miles, with three complete stops for traffic lights. In traffic this car would average 24 mpg, and highway cruising at 65/70 mph would give a consistent 28 mpg. We also made several spot checks on acceleration performance and, despite the lean jets, the performance was substantially identical to that reported here. However, don't get us wrong—most drivers would be well advised to use standard jets at all times. With the lean jets, the warm-up time is longer and the slight gain in economy (about 3 mpg) isn't worth the risk of burned exhaust valves at a low mileage.

Our stock test car recorded a low of 22 mpg and a high of 25. Overdrive, which is optional, of course, would restore the gas mileage to Mobilgas values. However, the standard 3.73:1 axle ratio is very well chosen and is an excellent compromise for good acceleration combined with economy. If you drive long distances at high speed, the overdrive would pay for itself, but frugal types can order a 3.54 axle for economy and save the hundred-odd dollars extra charge.

The much-revised engine, with overhead valves and a heavier crankshaft, is a tremendous improvement over the old L-head unit. It displaces 170 cu in., the same as two very competitive compacts, both rated at 101 bhp. Frankly, we were very suspicious when Studebaker rated this new engine at 112 bhp. If a car has an axle ratio well chosen for best possible top speed, its timed high speed runs are a definite and accurate guide to its true horsepower. And the Lark proved itself completely in

this test. The car is a good 10 mph faster than last year, and we might mention that our best timed run of 92.5 mph was made with the needle indicating 95. On several occasions we had the needle almost touching an indicated 100 mph, on a level road. But it takes a long, straight stretch of road to do it.

Acceleration times always reflect the effect of power-to-weight ratio and here again we got proof of the extra power. The zero to 60 mph time is a good 4 seconds quicker than last year. And zero to 60 in 14.0 seconds is mighty respectable performance for a small car that isn't as light as some of its opposition.

As a further check it might be of interest to mention that an engine's torque, or low speed pulling power, is directly and accurately shown by the Tapley meter we use. The only test we have available for direct comparison was a 1960 Lark with 4.10 axle and overdrive. Our 1961 test car recorded almost exactly the same Tapley pull readings in first, 2nd, and high as last year, despite

its 3.73 axle. Thus, reversing our thoughts, we can say that a 4.10 axle in the 1961 should produce 10% better pulling power readings than shown here. Coincidentally, this is very close to the added torque claimed by Studebaker for this new ohv engine.

In short, we were very much impressed with this new version of an "old" engine, whose ancestry dates back to the original Champion of 1939. We were even more impressed by the fact that, as we said in the beginning, fuel consumption is no worse. Actually, every trial we made indicates that fuel consumption has definitely been reduced and, in view of the vastly stepped-up performance, Studebaker engineers have accomplished the impossible. Incidentally, this engine is smooth and vibration-free at all normally used speeds. It shudders a little if you get down below 15 mph in high but this is a ridiculous way to drive anyway, particularly when 2nd gear is high enough to be useful, instead of one of those annoying 2:1 ratios found in so many cars of this size.

(In some cars a drop down from high to 2nd doubles the engine speed.) The engine runs up to 5100 rpm without valve float; this is 63 mph (67 indicated) in 2nd gear.

A perfectionist might find one slight flaw in this engine, so we'll mention it. There is just a trace of tappet noise, if you listen carefully, in comparison with the older engine—at least we thought this was so. Very few owners will ever notice it, we are certain, and, frankly, we would much rather hear the tappets (the mechanical type are used in the Lark) than face the noise problems associated with hydraulic units after 50,000 miles, or so.

The Lark six scores heavily over the V-8 version in the handling department. The steering is a little slow (4.4 turns), but this can be misleading because the gear gives a variable ratio and when only slight steering corrections are necessary, the action is commendably quick. And, because the 6-cylinder engine weighs about 250 lb less than the V-8, we enjoyed the benefit of much

lighter steering, along with considerably less understeer.

We thought the riding qualities were excellent and though the heavier Lark V-8 should ride better than the six, we were unable to detect much difference, unless one considers the long wheelbase (113 in.) Lark V-8 Cruiser tested by *Car Life* in March. In general, the Lark has the "feel" of a much heavier car and we suspect some of this advantage can be traced to the fact that Studebaker uses a rigid, separate frame rather than unit construction. While both types have advantages and disadvantages, there is no denying that a frame underneath

transmits less road noise and vibration to the passengers.

Our test car was one of the Deluxe models, an imposing name for a plain-Jane, standard 2-door sedan. However, the interior decor is neat and serviceable without being stark. If you want to pay a little more, the Regal version may be the answer. These models are beautifully finished inside and out, and the two-door sedan with the new-for-1961 roof and rear quarter panels was favored by several of our staff as being particularly good looking.

This brings up another point that pertains to all Larks,

namely, the high seating position. Although the 1961 cars are lower by one inch, the chair-height seats give comfortable seating and it is amazing to note the visibility advantage of sitting up a little higher than in most late-model cars. Maybe it was just us, but we didn't feel quite as hemmed-in, in heavy bumper-to-bumper traffic.

Studebaker has done a wonderful job of pepping up the Lark 6, in fact, almost too good—for this model almost makes the V-8 option superfluous. However, some people still want zero to 60 in 10 seconds, and the V-8 will do it for them. ∎

CAR LIFE ROAD TEST

LARK 6

SPECIFICATIONS

List price	$1935
Price, as tested	1935
Curb weight, lb	2910
Test weight	3200
distribution, %	55/45
Tire size	6.00-15
Tire capacity, lb	3484
Brake lining area	147
Engine type	6 cyl, ohv
Bore & stroke	3.0 x 4.0
Displacement, cc	2780
cu in.	169.6
Compression ratio	8.50
Bhp @ rpm	112 @ 4500
equivalent mph	92.1
Torque, lb-ft	154 @ 2000
equivalent mph	41.0

GEAR RATIOS

4th ( ), overall	n.a.
3rd (1.00)	3.73
2nd (1.63)	6.18
1st (2.61)	9.70

DIMENSIONS

Wheelbase, in.	108.5
Tread, f and r.	57.4/56.6
Over-all length, in.	175.0
width	71.4
height	56.5
equivalent vol, cu ft	408
Frontal area, sq ft	22.4
Ground clearance, in.	6.1
Steering ratio, o/a	22.0
turns, lock to lock	4.4
turning circle, ft	37.5
Hip room, front	59.5
Hip room, rear	59.0
Pedal to seat back, max	41.0
Floor to ground	13.5
Luggage vol, cu ft	16.5

PERFORMANCE

Top speed (3rd), mph	90.0
best timed run	92.5
3rd ( )	
2nd (5100)	63
1st (5100)	40

FUEL CONSUMPTION

Normal range, mpg	22/25

ACCELERATION

0-30 mph, sec	4.4
0-40	6.9
0-50	10.2
0-60	14.0
0-70	19.5
0-80	27.0
0-100	
Standing ¼ mile	19.2
speed at end	69

PULLING POWER

3rd, lb/ton @ mph	200 @ 50
2nd	350 @ 42
1st	490 @ 25
Total drag at 60 mph, lb	160

SPEEDOMETER ERROR

30 mph, actual	30.0
60 mph	56.5
90 mph	88.5

CALCULATED DATA

Lb/hp (test wt)	29.6
Cu ft/ton mile	90.0
Mph/1000 rpm	20.5
Engine revs/mile	2930
Piston travel, ft/mile	1950
Car Life wear index	57.2

ACCELERATION & COASTING

SS¼

3rd

2nd

1st

MPH — ELAPSED TIME IN SECONDS

STUDEBAKER Hawk

Since the winging Hawk's a full four-seater in the G.T. tradition, it should lure buyers who want both space and sport — made in the U.S.A.

► Studebaker-Packard's contribution to the American automotive industry's current ornithomania was hatched in 1953 with the then-revolutionary concept of a sleek, Raymond Loewy-designed, quasi-G.T. coupe. Since then the original Starliner has undergone annual name and plumage changes so that in its 1961 edition it no longer remains a fledgling but a fully flight-tested Hawk.

The Italianesque body, which was chosen for exhibit at New York's Museum of Modern Art when it was conceived, has withstood the rigors of time and facelifts and is still distinctively good looking. The engine-turned dashboard suggests the Cord as do the starkly functional, round, white-on-black instruments. A tachometer commands an imposing place, matching the speedometer right in front of the driver, but has no indicated redline. Hand controls for heater blowers, wipers, lights and such are convenient. The side ventilators are continued from earlier models and continue to rate a round of applause for their ability to provide cool, fresh air directly to the driver's or passenger's feet. The door-mounted ashtray on the driver's side is inconvenient to use, accessibility being blocked by the steering wheel. The flat floor enables owners to whisk out the small pebbles that seem to be standard equipment on every car without hurdling a door sill and the foot-operated windshield washer activates the wipers too when depressed fully. After a little familiarization you stop squirting the windshield when you want to dim the headlights.

The curiously-bent shift lever is handy and visibility all-around is good except for the slight blind spot caused by the larger-than-current-practice windshield posts. The Hawk was one of the few cars to resist the temptation to go to wrap-around windshields and thus is back in style today after others have abandoned them. Leg room is good, partly due to the squashed-circle steering wheel, and the pedals are placed for easy heel-and-toeing. The seats are attractive but we found them less comfortable than they look. The forward edge could use considerable inclination upward and the seat cushion needs more padding to achieve the bucket effect promised but not delivered by the shape. Rear seat room is more than enough for two, although legroom for the left-hand passenger diminishes sharply when the driver's

seat is fully rearward. The latter could use another half-inch or so of travel to satisfy long-legged chauffeurs. For those who yearn for features of the sports coupe of yesteryear in a modern guise, the Frank Hilker Studebaker dealership, 845 Halstead Street, Chicago Heights, Illinois has a solution. They are offering a "Bearcat Kit" to install a rumble seat in the Hawk or Studebaker Lark, priced at about $400.

The automatic choke on the four-barrel carb speeds warm-up and an idle of about 800 is par. The clutch operates smoothly and without undue pressure, although as shifts are made at increasing revs, the pressure goes up proportionally. First gear engages without a murmur and thanks to the limited-slip rear end, near-full-bore starts can be made even on wet pavement or sand. The H-pattern of the four-speed, all-synchro box is not easily learned. More than one C/D tester found himself doing a lot of driving in neutral while attempting to sort out the gates. If the driver takes his time, the shifting is almost instinctive, but fast shifts give unpredictable results, surprising in view of the faultless performance of the same Borg-Warner box in the Corvette. A lock-out for reverse would be desirable, but is not essential.

While the car we tested was undercoated we found the Hawk transferring considerable road noise into the cockpit. The testing, incidentally, included 4277 miles over a wide range of operating conditions. We found that steady pounding along at high speed caused the engine to require a quart of oil about every 500 miles although this appetite virtually disappeared after the odometer passed the 6600 mile mark; the car had about 3400 miles on it when we picked it up.

Kickback through the steering wheel on rough roads required the driver's attention although the power-assisted steering minimized effort. Around smoothly paved curves the Hawk fairly zoomed, its initial understeering tendency becoming more neutral as speeds increased. On rough, twisty back roads the car was still enjoyable to drive although corrections and the 4.6 turns lock-to-lock kept the driver's arms in a pinwheel of activity. Cruising at 70, 75, 80 or just about any speed you dare choose is effortless. Cross wind effects are negligible and cockpit ventilation is good without the car becoming a cave of winds.

The engine's torque and the choice of gears will satisfy even the most automatic-shift-oriented "driver." The engine will throttle down to a near idle in fourth and still pull away to over 110 mph in an inexorable whoosh. First-gear starts from a standstill will require skillful play of the clutch release and gas pedal as the cog is quite high; it will propel the car to almost 60 mph. For those who appreciate it, the power combination is well-suited to full-scale use. Even with such performance, economy doesn't suffer and is in fact very good for the kind of driving Hawks are intended for.

Pedal pressures are reduced considerably by the power-assisted brakes and stopping is quick although there is some loss of progressive brake application. An educated toe is advised for the best (that is, the least embarrassing) results. Hard braking causes the softly-sprung front end to dip considerably but control remains firmly in the driver's hands.

The Hawk, a pacesetter in the American industry's trend toward grand touring cars, held tremendous promise when it was introduced. For a while it appeared as if it was matching in the G.T. field Corvette's progress in the American sports car endeavor. The Hawk had all the potential of becoming an excellent and genuine G.T. machine, but it was never fully exploited. Perhaps what was lacking was the S-P equivalent of Corvette's secret ingredient, Duntov. It's still not too late for the Hawk to fulfill its stated role as "the first American car in the true G.T. tradition . . ." As it stands it's extremely capable—and strong competition for the new bucket-seated upstarts in its field.   —C/D

Wide-swinging doors and the flat floor add convenience to the Hawk's distinctive styling and designed-for-driving cockpit and performance.

The "air scoop" on the hood may not be functional, but everything else below and behind it is. The basic Hawk body was first introduced in 1953.

ROAD TEST

STUDEBAKER Hawk

Price as tested: $3384.98 ($2650 basic)

Manufacturer: Studebaker-Packard Corp.
South Bend 27, Indiana

ENGINE:

Displacement	289 cu in, 4737 cc
Dimensions	Eight cyl, 3.56 in bore, 3.63 in stroke
Valve gear	Pushrod in-line overhead valves
Compresion ratio	8.8 to one
Power (SAE)	225 bhp @ 4500 rpm
Torque	305 lb-ft @ 3000 rpm
Usable range of engine speeds	900-5300 rpm
Corrected piston speed @ 4500 rpm	2690 fpm
Fuel recommended	Regular
Mileage	14-21 mpg
Range on 18-gallon tank	250-380 miles

CHASSIS:

Wheelbase	120.5 in
Tread	F 57.4, R 56.6 in
Length	204.0 in
Ground clearance	6.9 in
Suspension: F, ind., coil, wishbones, anti-roll bar; R, rigid axle, asymmetrical leaf springs.	
Turns, lock to lock	4.6
Turning circle diameter between curbs	41 ft
Tire and rim size	6.70 x 15, 15 x 4½K
Pressures recommended	F 24, R 20 psi; 30 psi for high speeds
Brakes; type, swept area	F 11, R 10 in drums; 281 sq in
Curb weight (full tank)	3620 lbs
Percentage on driving wheels	46%

DRIVE TRAIN:

Gear	Synchro?	Ratio	Step	Overall	Mph per 1000 rpm
Rev	No	2.26	—	7.48	—10.8
1st	Yes	2.20		7.28	11.1
			33%		
2nd	Yes	1.66		5.49	14.7
			27%		
3rd	Yes	1.31		4.33	18.7
			31%		
4th	Yes	1.00		3.31	24.4

Final Drive Ratios: 3.31 to one std., 3.07, 3.54 optional.

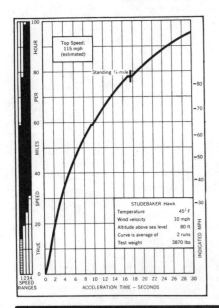

Graph:

Top Speed: 115 mph (estimated)

Standing ¼-mile

STUDEBAKER Hawk
Temperature 45°F
Wind velocity 10 mph
Altitude above sea level 80 ft
Curve is average of 2 runs
Test weight 3870 lbs

Y-axis: SPEED — MILES PER HOUR (TRUE MPH), 0 20 40 60 80 100; (INDICATED MPH) 30 40 50 60 70 80
X-axis: ACCELERATION TIME — SECONDS, 0 2 4 6 8 10 12 14 16 18 20 22 24 26 28 30
1234 SPEED RANGES

STUDEBAKER Hawk

GRAN TURISMO HAWK

The stylists at Studebaker have come up with a "custom" car which they hope will recapture their share of the prestige car market. The 1962 Hawk has been extensively restyled in, we understand, a hurry-up program. The end result resembles a Thunderbird greenhouse atop the original Loewy body with a Mercedes-type grille. Yet, for all its seeming copying of other cars, the Hawk has a very distinct aura about it. Especially distinctive is the dashboard, intelligently laid out with a full complement of instruments, including an optional mechanical tachometer. The surrounding fascia is of simulated wood.

Headroom in the rear has been increased over the previous models. The fins have been removed from the rear fenders where, for several post-Loewy years, they once were an addition.

Inside appointments include bucket seats with a reclining mechanism. Between them, as another option, projects a white knob-topped lever. At the other end of the stick is Borg-Warner's fine 4-speed, all-synchro gearbox. The ohv 6-cyl. is available for the first time.

STUDEBAKER HAWK

Wheelbase (in.)	120.5
Over-all length	204.0
Width	71.3
Weight (lb.)	3000
Brake area (sq. in.) (V-8: 172.8)	146.4

Engine: In-line 6-cyl., 170 cu. in. (3.0 in. bore x 4.0 in. stroke), 8:1 compression ratio. **Optional:** V-8, ohv, 259 cu. in. (3.56 x 3.25), 8.25:1; 289 cu. in. (3.56 x 3.63).

Horsepower: 112 @ 4500 rpm	Torque: 154 @ 2000 rpm
Optional: 180 @ 4500 rpm	260 @ 2800 rpm
210 @ 4500 rpm	300 @ 2800 rpm

Transmission: 3-speed manual (3-speed automatic optional; 4-speed, all-synchro manual optional on Hawk V-8)

Axle Ratio(s): 3.73 (3.07, 3.31, 3.54, 4.10 and 4.56 optional)

GRAN TURISMO HAWK

STUDEBAKER Lark & Daytona

STUDEBAKER LARK & DAYTONA	
Wheelbase (in.) (4-door & wagon: 113.0)	109.0
Over-all length (4-door sedan: 188.0)	184.0
Width	71.4
Weight (lb.)	2900
Brake area (sq. in.) (V-8: 172.8)	146.4

Engine: In-line 6-cyl., 170 cu. in. (3.0 in. bore x 4.0 in. stroke), 8:1 compression ratio. **Optional:** V-8, ohv, 259 cu. in. (3.56 x 3.25), 8.25:1; 289 cu. in. (3.56 x 3.63).

Horsepower: 112 @ 4500 rpm   **Torque:** 154 @ 2000 rpm
Optional: 180 @ 4500 rpm (259 V-8) 260 @ 2800 rpm
210 @ 4500 rpm (289 V-8) 300 @ 2800 rpm

Transmission: 3-speed manual (overdrive or 3-speed automatic optional)

Axle Ratio(s): 3.73 (3.07, 3.31, 3.54, 4.10 and 4.56 optional)

Lark, for 1962, answers the past criticism of those who claimed the car was too short: It not only *looks* longer, it *is* longer (184 in. o/a for '62 vs. 175 in. for '61) and the new package is topped off with an entirely new roof line in the hardtop models. This new "greenhouse" reminds many of a Mercedes-Benz, as will the new grille, a massive affair thrusting its way ahead of the car. As a cut in a direction of the German firm (whose products Studebaker distributes in this country), the rear end of the car has been redesigned and now features round taillights and no fins. Trunk capacity has been improved by the additional overhang and by lifting the rear line of the lid several inches.

Mechanically, like most of the '62s, the Lark is unchanged. A small, ohv 6-cyl., a medium-sized V-8 and a big (289-cu.-in.) V-8 are still offered, with horsepower ratings from 112 to 210; not high but quite economical.

In the current fashion, Lark will have a sporty model with bucket seats. Sensibly named, it is called the Daytona, presumably after Lark's various successes there in economy runs.

LARK CRUISER 4-DOOR SEDAN

NEW for '62

STUDEBAKER'S SILVER HAWK

ALL THAT SHINES IS NOT CHROME

Although most American cars are inclined to be big and brassy, Studebaker's Silver Hawk almost makes grade as a good sports-cum-touring car.

WHEELS FULL ROAD TEST

By PETER HALL

F post Second World War sales figures are any indication, the American car market is a gold mine for sports cars, and "sporting" high performance sedans.

The British Motor Corporation has earned tens of millions of dollars for Britain because of the demand in America for its MG and Austin-Healey sports cars.

The United States has been a very benevolent uncle to the shareholders of the Jaguar company and it has done much to keep Britain's Standard-Triumph group afloat with its continual demand for Triumph TR2, TR3 and now, TR4 sports cars.

The wonder of it all is not that Americans have demanded sports cars so consistently and in such numbers, but rather that the American car makers have done so little to satisfy this multi-million dollar segment of their own market.

It is only in the last few years that any American car maker has made any serious effort at all to make sports cars. Neither Ford nor Chevrolet can have any complaints with the public acceptance and the undoubted profits of their respective Thunderbird and Corvette sports and touring cars.

Only one other maker seems to have done anything about satisfying the sports-minded or "specialist" car lovers in America. And that is the

Basically, the Silver Hawk is a design of many years standing, although various modifications have modernised it from time to time.

Studebaker-Packard Corporation.

And their efforts seem to have been due more to expediency than a determined from-scratch effort to crack the sporting minded market.

The car? The Studebaker Hawk.

The evolution of the Hawk as we know it in Australia is quite a story.

In 1953, Raymond Loewy, the great American designer whose name went round the world in 1947 for his radical coming-or-going Studebaker, designed one of the most beautiful cars ever to come from an American factory.

A low - slung comparatively de-chromed coupe, it seemed destined to revive the then sagging Stude-

Profile view of the Silver Hawk shows its clean lines to advantage. Not very finny, it is one of the best looking of the American-designed cars.

baker fortunes. But several things happened which, added together, nearly made Loewy's beautiful coupe the chief cause of Studebaker going under altogether.

For a start, Studebaker rushed the '53 coupe into production and it quickly gained a reputation for being a poorly-built motor car. Again, the demand for coupes, even such a good looking one as this Studebaker, was not sufficient to keep the company out of the red. And the four-door sedans and station wagons Studebaker built on the coupe design were flops. The coupe was beautiful, the

others were a mess from a design point of view.

Later, Studebaker-Packard (they are now amalgamated) saved its skin — and got well and truly back on the dividend list with the compact Studebaker Lark. But the company kept the coupe design, and with various modifications and embellishments turned it into the Studebaker Hawk.

For a time, a few Hawks, and even one or two of the now discontinued supercharged model, the Golden Hawk, drifted into Australia. But sales were somewhat restricted by a price tag nearing £2900.

Then, late in 1960, the old established Melbourne firm, Canada Cycle and Car Co Pty Ltd, signed an agreement with Studebaker-Packard to assemble the Studebaker range at Canada Cycle's small plant at Tottenham, near Melbourne.

First models off the line were the Lark and the Lark cruiser (the automatic model) and a Lark station wagon. They caught on rapidly at their heavily reduced prices, despite the credit squeeze, the Canada Cycle were ready to go ahead with the more ambitious project of assembling the Hawk.

The first Hawks came off the Tottenham assembly line a few months ago, and they have been well received.

They caught on so well indeed for a limited production car, thanks to a large degree to a whopping £600 price reduction over the imported model, that Canada Cycle did not have the need or the opportunity to register one as a demonstration car.

But one was eventually registered for Canada Cycle's governing director Mr Len Buxton, and yours truly got the chance of testing it. Mr Buxton has been a motorist for many years and has closely guarded the number plate he had on his first car. Hence the number shown in the photographs of the test car — 401. He has lost count of the number of

Instrumentation is simple and very much to the point. Lever on the right is automatic transmission selector — manual on special order only.

To give good access to the rear seats, the front squabs jack-knife neatly. The doors are very wide, without wrap around screen dog-leg.

cars it has adorned and he intends keeping it for many more.

In the United States, the Studebaker Hawk can be had with several different engines and transmissions. You can have an economical 112 bhp six or either of two V8 engines, both of them offered with two or four barrel carburettors.

And you can have either a three-speed automatic gearbox or a fully-synchronised four-speed gearbox with a floor-mounted change lever. A limited slip differential and a rev-counter are among other options available in America.

But for the Australian market, the Studebaker "option" range has been rationalised. The six cylinder engine is not available here at all, either in the Larks or the Hawk. The Lark is fitted with the smaller of the two V8 engines and has a normal two-barrel carby. The Hawk has the top engine of the range —the 289 cu in V8 complete with four-barrel carburetter and a thumping 225 bhp.

The transmission has been standardised on the Hawk in this country also. The only one offered here is the automatic. The limited slip diff is not available except on special order, nor is the four speed gearbox.

The automatic's ratios were well chosen for the engine's power curve

and there was little need to over-ride the automatic brain — except, perhaps to conserve brakes on long downhill runs or maintain the transmission in intermediate gear for sustained medium speed cornering when the driver would want to be in the position of being able to deliver maximum power to the back wheels the instant he depressed the accelerator, and not wait a second or two for the gearbox to do it for him.

Around the city, particularly in peak traffic, the Hawk's automatic transmission, of course, was at its best. Almost completely relaxed, the driver can potter from traffic jam to traffic jam with a minimum of nerve strain and his only physical effort being a bit of pedal and quite a bit of arm work.

If the Studebaker Hawk is really intended to be a sports car, it falls down quite badly in this one respect — steering.

The turning circle is enormous (45 feet) in these days of narrow turning locks and to go from one lock to the other requires no less than six complete spins of the wheel.

Of course, this very low geared steering does have its advantages. With its massive cast iron V8 engine keeping the big front wheels well on the ground and no power assistance

provided, the Studebaker would be darn hard to turn if it had a genuine sports car's direct, high geared steering.

Again on long, well graded highways —the sort of roads most American Hawk drivers probably use exclusively, its steering system is quite adequate and very relaxing. The car keeps winging along in a straight line with only an occasional hand movement on the driver's part. It is only when you get into trials' territory or try to take a mountain circuit as if you were hell-bent to win the Targia Florio do you get really upset about the excessive windmill work you have to do on the steering wheel.

I do think Studebaker could have compromised a bit on this one. I doubt if around about four to four and a half turns from lock to lock would make the car excessively heavy to move about at crawling pace and it would certainly give the Hawk much more character on a really vigorous drive.

The power from the V8 engine is tremendous and the deep, throbbing note emanating from the twin exhaust system — a song in any true man's ear.

Start the motor, listen to the music, slip the selector lever to D and floor the accelerator. Then you will find this Stude really is made of iron muscles.

It would probably pass the ton in less than 30 seconds, but the front wheels on the test car were not in perfect balance and developed a rather frightening hammering at about 85 which grew steadily worse until the car was at its top speed. Two top speed runs were enough for me, so the 0-100 mph acceleration time goes unrecorded.

The conventional springing provides an unconventional firm ride on the Hawk that gives you confidence. Roll on corners is negligible and so its the car's tendency to understeer.

Brakes are a real surprise. For an American car, the Hawk is adequately braked. Fade was negligible and the broad pedal needed little foot pressure to bring the car screeching to very quick stops indeed, from any speed at all. There was no power assistance on this car, just great big drums, well finned and stuck well out from the wheels where they get the chance to cool off quickly. Just about every other American car maker could profitably do a bit of research, or spying at whatever part of the Studebaker factory where the brakes are designed.

Fittings were adequate — more than adequate, in fact, in the instrument department. The only grizzles there were fitting of a huge clock instead of a rev counter and bad placing of the headlight dipper switch under the driver's heel.

Finish could have been better, but considering the big price saving on the imported model and the short time the local assembly plant has been going, it was passable.

Not a sports car, perhaps, the Australian-made Studebaker is at least an exciting high performance. And, except for the fins (Loewy never put them there) very handsome indeed. #

wheels ROAD TEST

TECHNICAL DETAILS

OF THE

SILVER HAWK

PERFORMANCE

TOP SPEED:

Fastest run	106 mph
Average of all runs	104.7 mph

MAXIMUM SPEED IN GEARS:

Low	52 mph
Intermediate	61 mph
Drive	106 mph

ACCELERATION:

Standing quarter mile;	
Fastest run	17.7 sec
Average of all runs	17.75 sec
0 to 30 mph	3.55 sec
0 to 40 mph	5.0 sec
0 to 50 mph	7.6 sec
0 to 60 mph	10.7 sec
0 to 70 mph	14.5 sec
0 to 80 mph	19.5 sec
20 to 40 mph	2.4 sec
30 to 50 mph	3.8 sec
40 to 60 mph	4.3 sec

GO-TO-WHOA:

0 to 60 to 0 mph	14.3 sec

SPEEDO ERROR:

Indicated	Actual
30 mph	24.9 mph
50 mph	43 mph
70 mph	61.1 mph

FUEL CONSUMPTION:

Overall (127 miles)	15.8 mpg

PRICE:

	£2295

TEST CAR FROM:

Canada Cycle & Car Co. Pty. Ltd., Latrobe Street, Melbourne.

SPECIFICATIONS

ENGINE:

Cylinders	8, vee formation
Bore and stroke	3.56 x 3.62 in
Cubic capacity	289 cu. in (4737 cc)
Compression ratio	7.5 to 1
Valves	pushrod, overhead
Carburettor	four barrel
Power at rpm	225 at 4500 rpm
Maximum Torque	305 ft lbs at 3000 rpm

TRANSMISSION:

Type	Three-speed Borg-Warner automatic

SUSPENSIONS:

Front	independent, coil springs
Back	semi-elliptic leaf springs
Shockers	telescopic

STEERING:

Type	cam and lever
turns, lock to lock	6¼
Circle	45 ft

BRAKES:

Type	drum

DIMENSIONS:

Wheelbase	10 ft 0½ in
Track, front	4 ft 9¾ in
Track, rear	4 ft 11⅛ in
Length	17 ft
Width	5 ft 11¾ in
Height	4 ft 7½ in

TYRES:

Size	6.70 x 15

WEIGHT:

Kerb	28½ cwt

CONTINUED FROM PAGE 28

Taking the Hawk over the same course we used for the Corvette and Thunderbird, I was disappointed in the way it handled. The supercharged power was lost in tight turns, since I was forced to get off the throttle in order to get the front end under control. The body leaned considerably through the turns, and the wheel felt sluggish in my hands. Recovery was not as rapid as I would have liked it, which meant taking the turns considerably slower than I did with the other cars.

Despite all this, however, the '57 Hawk is an improvement over the '56. Studebaker engineers have done much to eliminate the handling problem by lightening the front end and adding the new variable-ratio steering that works through a gear arrangement. This is quite an improvement over last year's car.

Then, too, Studebaker's new "Twin Traction" delivers engine power to the "gripping" wheel on slippery streets (or to the inside wheel on turns), giving the Hawk more roadability than before. The Twin-Traction differential is optional at extra cost.

Studebaker craftsmanship has been something to boast about for years, and this fact is evident in the workmanship on the '57 Golden Hawk. I noticed this especially with the brakes—best of the three cars tested. I had very little brake fade, except on the panic stop at 100 mph. The quick stop was smooth despite our speed, and while there was a certain amount of fade the recovery was exceptionally rapid.

Finned drums, which shed heat by allowing cool air to circulate around the lining, was the answer here. After the panic stop I noticed some fade; but it was gone by the time I turned the car around and tried the brakes again.

Summing it up, I believe all three cars are a credit to American styling and engineering. I cannot recommend one over the other because public acceptance depends on individual likes and needs. The Corvette has done well toward capturing the true sports-car enthusiast. The Thunderbird ranks as an "in-betweener", with an appealing emphasis on both the sports-car angle and passenger-car comfort. The Golden Hawk, by the same token has a big bill to fill by appealing to family needs as well as sports enthusiasts.

In all three cases, I feel that these three cars have a definite place in American motoring. They give evidence of America's successful venture into sports car styling; a venture that, only a few years ago, was surrounded by skepticism. But it has gone on with constant improvements that promise an even greater future. ●

OH, WHAT A LARK

CONTINUED FROM PAGE 43

I was delighted to see that the transmission hump in front in the Lark sedan was not so big that it precluded me from carrying two companions. With many of the bigger autos nobody but a child can sit in the centre "hot seat".

The rear seat is a different matter. To make it seem that you've a lot of knee-room here, the design boys simply cut the depth of the back seat by roughly half, so that you sit, in effect, on your bottom and nothing else. Very naughty, this.

Out on the road it's difficult to guess what kind of suspension keeps the Lark so nicely remote from the road. Later, when you crawl under the car, you see the front end is held up by coil springs and wishbones with double-acting shockers enclosed by the springs . A heavy anti-sway bar attached to the wishbone on each side performs unbelievably good service on hard corners.

At rear are two faithful semi-elliptic leaf springs damped by inclined double-acting shockers. Nothing unconvential, front or rear, but the system does the job.

I pushed the Lark through several hard corners under "kick-down" acceleration until, under great protest, the rear end broke traction. I corrected the resulting dry slide with one hand on the wheel. That's how easy it is to control this car.

It doesn't require any courage on my part to say that this is the best-handling American car I've ever driven.

A number of times I stood on the brakes at speeds above 30 m.p.h.

and the Stude hauled to a dead stop with startling ease. Not equipped with a Tapley meter at the time, I would have betted the Lark could ring up 96-98 per cent efficiency on any kind of metal surface.

Certainly, with a speed potential in the 115 m.p.h. zone, you need stoppers of this calibre. Brake lining area, at 172.4 sq. in., doesn't seem overmuch measured against such velocities, but . . . well, it stops!

The key to the verve and vivacity of the Lark is, of course, its power. To us Anglo-Saxons, raised on traditions of moderation in everything, it almost seems downright vulgar to be able to plant your hoof on the accelerator at a traffic light and hit 30 m.p.h. in just 3.6 seconds. Maybe it IS vulgar, but I love it.

Performance in the middle speed ranges is extraordinary, too. In some cars the seconds between 30 and 50 m.p.h. seem like an eternity (especially when there's a semi-trailer coming at you as you're passing another car), but in the Lark they're effortless and unnoticed.

Altogether, the Lark is a revolution, and a revelation.

If you're interested in owning one you should be warned right now that any one of the three models available at the time of writing will cost you twice as much as a Holden.

Prices are: Four-door sedan £2,585 (including tax), two-door hardtop £2,620, station wagon £2,785.

Optional equipment includes Twin Traction "non-slip" differential, power brakes (which you don't need), air conditioning, and the automatic hill-holder park lock for models other than those fitted with automatic transmission. #

LARK'S TRIM NEW FEATHERS

CONTINUED FROM PAGE 94

Riding qualities of the Studebaker are better this year. Formerly, the springing was quite hard—marvellous for the budding Fangios, but hardly necessary. The '60 and '61 Larks were very stable cars, but a bit truck like in the riding department.

This year, they have altered the spring rates and fitted softer shockers. I think the move is a definite improvement.

On fast corners, there is a predictable amount of body and a substantial tendency to understeer. But with all that power and reasonably well-balanced weight, the Lark gives no bad moments.

Although there seems to be no change in specifications, the brakes were decidedly better. Sure, they faded after a few hard stops from near maximum speeds, but recovery was quick, pedal pressures reasonably light and I found no tendency to veer from the straight line of safe braking.

In fact, it seems, someone has been doing a bit of experimenting with lining and drum materials. What they have come up with is a decided improvement.

Finish shows another major step in the direction of ultimate high quality. Indeed, this model Stude can match it on this score with just about anything in its size class, if you don't mind doors that are a bit hard to shut and don't quite have the right "clunk". As far as that goes, I have a suspicion the Studebaker makes a more honest noise.

All told, the slight price rise of £20 seems more than justified—the new Lark is a darn good car with strong claims to be the best value, pound for pound, in the V8 class. #

DOMESTIC CAR OF THE YEAR

CT&T's pick of the domestic car of the year is based on the same principles used in determining the imported product: the automobile judged to be the best example of good design and customer value.

Our award for 1961 goes to Studebaker's Lark, a product of what might be called the Outer Two of the North American automobile industry. Studebaker-Packard's whole plant would probably fit into the board room of one of the Big Three complexes, yet its comparatively modest physical size has not made the Studebaker-Packard firm's aims any smaller or less worthwhile.

Actually, the very fact that Studebakers aren't produced in daily acre lots may well explain why the Lark

STUDEBAKER LARK

DOMESTIC CAR OF THE YEAR

receives our domestic Car of the Year award. With production limited, inspection and adjustment time is increased on every car and Studebaker has made the most of this. The Lark is a sound, solid design. But we suspect that its dominant virtue is the care and special pains taken to ensure reliability, to avoid the slipshod mass-production techniques which have sent more than a few infuriated domestic customers scurrying off to see their imported car dealers.

An interesting sidelight in proof of Studebaker's attention to quality is its reputation as the domestic manufacturer with the lowest incidence of "lemons" per 100 units. A visit to Studebaker-Packard's compact plant in Hamilton, Ont. reveals first-hand the many extra steps taken to build in longevity at the factory, rather than relying on patch-ups at the dealer level. The entire body shell is dipped in a rust-preventative solution before painting, as one example. Cars leaving the production line are given thorough final inspections - sometimes by Gordon Grundy, President of Studebaker-Packard of Canada who occasionally strolls through the plant on spot checks of his own.

The end result of Studebaker-Packard's conscientious approach is a car deserving of owner confidence, one not likely to be tied up in repeated trips back to the dealer for adjustments. In short, a car offering good customer value.

A Lark took first overall in the Shell-B.C.I.T.F. Trans Canada Rally last May, and in compact races over the past two years, the unprepossessing Lark has gained more than its share of wins. Yet this is not by any stretch of the imagination a sporting car and Studebaker is wise enough not to make such claims for it. It's a pleasant, honest, medium-sized automobile designed for versatile use under North American conditions. There are flashier cars doing the same thing, many cheaper to buy initially. But CT&T is happy to present its domestic Car of the Year award for 1961 to Studebaker-Packard's Lark as a tribute to its all-round qualities and in recognition of this firm's sincere efforts to raise the standards of domestic automobile manufacture.

62 LARK
BY STUDEBAKER

CAR LIFE
Road Test

Studebaker Lark
Daytona

LENGTH AND LUXURY have been added to the Studebaker Lark this year. Over-all length has been stretched at least 9 in. on all models, while greater luxury is featured in a new sport series, the Daytona. In our opinion, the increase in bumper-to-bumper dimensions improves the Lark both esthetically and functionally. The car has had a stubby rear deck that not only looked awkward but also allowed very little trunk space. While the passenger compartment was—and is—quite roomy, the exterior was too compact! The new sheet metal is concentrated at the rear to correct these faults.

No, we're not going to admonish Studebaker for adding overhang and producing a "bigger smaller" car. We feel the longer deck is an honest change for the better. And the 1962 Lark is still within anybody's definition of "compact," measuring 184 in. in 2-door body types and 188 in 4-door styles.

The other novelty for 1962, the Daytona, is a jazzy sport model offered in 2-door hardtop and convertible form. Special interior trim distinguishes this series.

The Daytona is available with any of Studebaker's power trains, a 6-cyl. of 112 bhp or a V-8 of 180, 195, 210 or 225 bhp, coupled to a 3-speed, 3-speed with overdrive, 4-speed (not available with 6-cyl. engine) or automatic transmission.

A white Daytona convertible with red and white trim will pace America's top racing drivers into action at this year's Indianapolis 500. Our test car was a duplicate of this honored vehicle in all but one respect; the Indy version will have the 225-bhp engine with 4-speed gearbox, while ours was the 180-bhp with automatic. We plan to test the hotter power train in a 1962 Hawk and felt a milder setup in the Daytona would enable us to present a broader over-all picture of Studebaker's current offerings.

The 180-bhp unit puts the Daytona in a price and

power bracket with the Buick Skylark, Oldsmobile Cutlass and Tempest V-8 Le Mans. And, in many ways, it's the same kind of car—compact but nicely finished, with more than enough engine output for normal driving conditions.

But there are important differences, too. Studebaker developed the original 1959 Lark from its older Champion and Commander models and much of these earlier designs lingers on in the Daytona.

To begin with, the car is quite heavy for its size. The Lark is the only compact with a separate body and frame. Add to this the bulk of a V-8 engine (created a decade ago for big car use) and the special bracing needed to support convertible bodywork and the result is a compact with a curb weight of 3530 lb., as much as most full-size automobiles.

We were particularly conscious of this heaviness because our Daytona didn't have power assists for either steering or brakes. Without them, the handling wasn't nearly as responsive as the over-all dimensions might suggest. The car would fit into a tight parking place but considerable effort was required to get it there.

Attempts at vigorous cornering also reminded us that this wasn't a very light car. Here, the difficulty wasn't just sheer weight but the concentration of so much of it at the front (58.8% of the total). Studebaker's V-8 powerplant contains a lot of cast iron and is shoved well forward in the Lark chassis. In tight turns, the front end of the test car plowed badly and the feeling of understeer was amplified by the wheel's positive centering action. To our pleasant surprise, though, body sway wasn't at all serious.

On the straight and level, the Daytona's avoirdupois showed to advantage. The weight tended to minimize the pitching often experienced in cars with short wheelbases and, despite fairly soft spring rates, the ride was stable and quiet at all speeds. Almost any road surface short of cracked asphalt could be taken swiftly and smoothly.

Fortunately, our Daytona was powered to overcome its bulk and proved quite brisk through its automatic gears. The 180-bhp V-8 displaces 259.2 cu. in. and has a single 2-barrel carburetor and an 8.5:1 compression ratio. Flexible and responsive, it gets along nicely on ▶

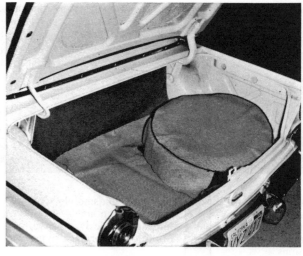

Studebaker Lark Daytona

moderate amounts of regular fuel. A 4-barrel carburetor and dual exhausts account for the 195-bhp option, while the 289-cu. in. Hawk engine is the basis of the 210- and 225-bhp units.

Lighter Larks, including the Daytona hardtop, will perform satisfactorily with the 6-cyl. powerplant but we

CONTINUED ON PAGE 100

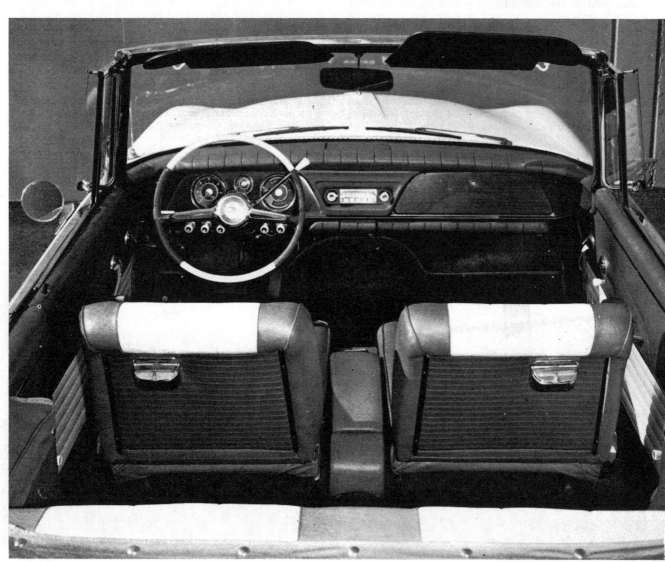

CT&T ROAD TEST

STUDEBAKER LARK DAYTONA

Speed to Spare in This Lively Compact

THE CAR

South Bend isn't too far from Detroit to feel the winds of change, and Studebaker-Packard entered 1962 knowing the sporty theme would be one of the year's major automotive trends. Their answer has been the Lark Daytona.

The Daytona, unlike many other U.S.-designed sporty compacts imported into Canada, is being built at Studebaker-Packard's Hamilton, Ontario plant. Following much the same pattern as others in its class, it offers a deluxe interior set-up featuring bucket seats and floor-mounted, four-speed manual transmission. Engine options range from a cooking, six-cylinder 112 hp rig to a scalding 225-hp V8. The long list of performance extras bigger brakes, heavy-duty suspension, a huskier clutch and limited slip differential.

Our test car, supplied courtesy of Glen Manor Motors of Toronto, carried the ultimate V-8 and virtually all of Studebaker's performance options.

TECHNICAL

Largest of the three Studebaker engine choices is the 289 cu. in. V-8, assisted by an optional 4-barrel carburetor that ups horsepower from 210 to 225. Bore and stroke are 3.0 x 3.25 in. respectively and torque is listed at 305 lbs. ft. at 3000 rpm. Compression ratio is 8.5 to 1. Suspension is conventional, by coil springs at front and leaf springs at rear. Transmission on our test car was the optional four-speed floor shift, but automatic is another option and standard equipment is a manual 3-speed fitting.

Studebaker still uses the body-on-frame method as opposed to widespread industry use of unit bodies. The advantage is a level floor instead of the step-down type, with more of a chair-type seating arrangement than unit-bodied cars can offer. Also retained are 15-inch wheels, when most of the competition has gone to 14 or even 13-inch sizes.

STYLING

The Lark's looks in '62 represent a vast improvement over earlier models, mostly because of added length at the rear and adoption of a few Mercedes bends up front. Still, in a field marked by extensive annual changes, what is basically a four year old design is beginning to show its age.

Workmanship and assembly on our test car bore up well under close inspection, though an exception was a jagged bit of trim on one door that cut a staff member's hand.

INTERIOR

Compared to CT&T's usual run of test cars, the Daytona's interior dimensions seemed vast on first acquaintance and we took a while to become accustomed to everything being proportionately further away. Once accepted, this greater size has definite advantages, both physical and psychological. There is enough room sideways, forward, up and back for the rangiest occupant, and all that space allows one to stretch out and relax in the grand manner on long trips. Since this is the type of car born for extended touring, space is a virtue where in an around-town car it would be a waste. For a compact, the Lark is remarkably roomy inside and excess space has been pared where it isn't needed anyway.

The "bucket type" seats installed in most sporting compacts have come under fire from purists, who dispute their claim to the term. If the word is meant to describe an enveloping shell that eliminates lateral motion and holds its occupant securely but comfortably, then the Daytona doesn't have bucket seats. If it merely signifies a separate, firmer-than-usual seat (and this seems to be Detroit's liberal interpretation of the phrase), then the Daytona does have bucket seats. Either way, these are far more comfortable than the traditional bench-type, and with safety belt fastened we found them comfortable without being restricting.

A small console lies between the front seats on the transmission tunnel, and this appears to be more of an ornamentation than a necessity since a proper glove compartment is provided on the dashboard. Luckily the dashboard also holds a pull-out ashtray; the tiny item mounted on the console is just too fussy for practical use.

Rear-seat comfort and legroom are first-rate, and while we haven't tested them all we doubt that many cars of the Lark's 109-inch wheelbase can match its interior dimensions. Pile carpeting covers the floor, and tasteful vinyl trim is used on door panels and headliner.

For a "sporting type" car, instrumentation seemed on the slight side. Aside from a circular speedometer dial, the only gauges are for fuel and temperature. A tachometer doesn't appear on the list of options. A

rich wood-grain finish and padded upper surface are attractive touches. The oval-shaped steering wheel allows a good look at the instruments and lots of room for the driver's legs. The centrally mounted gearshift lever, mounted on the driveshaft tunnel just ahead of the console, is tall and surmounted by a hefty plastic ball easily gripped and shifted.

DRIVING

Before drawing any conclusions from our test, perhaps it should be noted that the car we tested had over 4,000 miles on the clock and was shod with snow tires at the rear. It had also just completed an arduous Winter Rally, arduous enough that the optional stiffer suspension had lost some of its rigidity. Performance figures consequently might be at variance with another car.

No expert is needed to pinpoint the Daytona's foremost characteristic as power, and with the tail-twisting take-off punch on hand we wondered if some other makers aren't overdoing it a bit in this department. Certainly the Daytona's 289 cubic inches are more than enough for any sane driver on public roads.

Going flat-out in a straight line is much the same in one car as another, but we did note tremendous gearbox flexibility; 40 mph in first, 65 in second and 80 in third gear. Due no doubt to the snow tires mounted on our test car, high speeds brought a fair amount of vibration but not from the robust V-8 engine, quiet and smooth in all ranges. This car could be driven at quite illegal highway speeds without even using fourth cog. Careful clutching was needed to avoid wheelspin on take-off, but this was about the only precaution required—aside from a close eye on the speedometer because of the ridiculous ease with which 80 mph is attained. Otherwise, the Daytona felt as docile as a standard Lark.

Ride, even with heavy-duty suspension, was hardly harsh yet free from the wallowing after-bounce so often cited as "typical Detroit". Body lean on corners is substantially less than that of standard Larks but enough to remind you that this is a big and heavy piece of machinery. Over rough roads the suspension did a good job of ironing out potholes and bumps, transferring little of the rough going into the passenger compartment, and the body was free of rattles and

groans. Under vigorous cornering the Daytona re-vealed real tenacity, although heavy acceleration out of turns brought about some sudden and alarming (at least from outside) fishtailing. But steering is far too slow for the rest of the car, and a trip over long stretches of winding road would be very tough on the arms. For the average driver's needs, the Lark's slow steering is probably acceptable. But the enthusiast would want something done about it.

The Daytona's beefier 11 x 2½-inch finned brakes are a madatory accessory to all that power, and came through our tests smoothly, without fade.

ECONOMY

Using premium fuel, our test car delivered an average of 21 miles per gallon in city and highway use. Gas tank capacity is 15 gallons, ensuring a range of about 300 miles between stops.

STORAGE SPACE

A big trunk with a low sill would seem adequate for the travelling needs of anything short of a small army, with artillery.

HEATING

One of the reasons we secretly enjoy testing big cars is the rapid and ample heating provided. The Day-tona, in spite of a rather intricate series of knobs and vents, gushed out warm air almost immediately in cold weather. Noise from the blower was obvious but not obtrusive.

LAST WORD

Our impression of the Daytona was that it is a burly, capable and exhilerating road car without any wild extremes, pro or con. With all that juice on tap it's comforting to feel that this car is as solid as a rock, yet comfortable enough to serve admirably in normal driving. True-blue driving enthusiasts will mourn the slow steering and lack of genuine sports car "feel", but American car buyers looking for something more responsive than the standard Detroit product will pro-bably find the Daytona just their cup of tea. And not to tramp on the feelings of the sports car set, it's this kind of buyer at whom the Daytona is aimed.

DATA & SPECIFICATIONS

Engine: V-8, water-cooled
Bore: 3.56 in.
Stroke: 3.25 in.
Piston displacement: 289 cu. in.
Compression ratio: 8.5 to 1.
Brake horsepower: 225 at 4500 rpm.
Torque: 305 lbs. ft. at 3000 rpm.
Transmission: 4 speeds forward, one reverse, syncromesh on second, third and fourth. **Gear ratios:** 1st., 2.42; 2nd., 1.92; 3rd., 1.51; 4th, 1:1.
Brakes: Drum-type, heavy-duty 11x2½-inch, finned.
Front suspension: Direct double-action shock absorbers mounted in coil springs.
Rear suspension: Sea leg mounted shock absorbers and 4-leaf springs asymmetric to axle.
Steering: 4½ turns, lock-to-lock.
Turning radius: 37½ ft.
Wheelbase: 109 in.
Overall length: 184 in.
Overall width: 71¼ in.
Overall height: 55¾ in.
Weight, unladen: 3015 lbs.

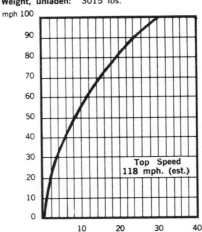

Top Speed 118 mph. (est.)

The Editor corners the compact and exceedingly manoeuvrable Daytona Lark.

A LARK THAT REALLY FLIES

Studebaker's V8
Daytona Hard Top
Special a
Compact Bombshell

BY GREGOR GRANT

PHOTOGRAPHY BY GEORGE PHILLIPS

INSOFAR as the average Detroit-built car goes it is ideal for North American conditions. It is roomy, comfortable, silent and possesses a performance far in excess of the requirement of Mr. and Mrs. John Doe. Strictly controlled limits on state highways, freeways and turnpikes make anything over 70 m.p.h. cruising a chancey and somewhat expensive business. Consequently the only performance factor which counts is the ability to accelerate from standstill up to the safe cruising speed as quickly as possible. With their big motors, even the lowest-priced U.S. automobile has a fairly useful getaway, but on wet roads only the provision of "twin-traction", or limited spin differential as we say in Europe, can provide the necessary grip to spinning rear wheels.

There are, of course, places where maximum speed can be used; such as certain trans-desert routes where patrol cars are few and far between and radar-timing non-existent. However, the large percentage of motor cars in America spend their time cruising between 55 and 65 m.p.h. and it is usually the owners of imported machines who take to the by-roads where, early on, they discovered that the products of Detroit were not exactly suited to sports car-style cornering—nor were brakes effective in mountainous regions unless one drove very moderately indeed.

Perhaps it is because South Bend, Indiana, is not in Detroit, Michigan, that the Studebaker-Packard concern have tended to break away from the normal conception of an American automobile.

Several years ago their Raymond Loewy-designed closed car was in direct contrast to the chromium-festooned gin-palaces of rival manufacturers. It took time, but others realized that Studebaker had something and this led to an outbreak of pseudo-Italian-styled vehicles which looked as though they had been conceived by the least able of Paris Left Bank impressionists. Sad to relate, the slinky Studebaker came in for "treatment", which spoiled the pure line and it became just another American automobile.

However, during the past year or so the stylish Hawk has once more put the Studebaker concern on the map, where good-looking motor cars are concerned, and the two-door Gran Turismo model has all the appeal of the original Loewy-automobile.

BY LAKE PLACID. The two-door Daytona Hard Top looks more a European than an American production. The fusion of Studebaker-Packard and Mercedes-Benz interests in the U.S.A. has caused a certain resemblance between the Daytona Lark and a Mercedes-Benz 220S.

AUTOSPORT, APRIL 20, 1962

With the Lark the corporation was one of the earliest in the compact field. As originally presented, this was a sensible saloon, without frills and not exactly an eye-catcher as regards appearance. Nevertheless, it did have individuality and with the V8 engine installed, it out-performed everything else in the compact field. Recently the Lark has been the subject of considerable modification, as well as the introduction of several body styles, including convertible, station wagon and hard top editions. To European eyes one of the most attractive versions is the Daytona Hard Top, an extremely comfortable and well-finished product which is also available in special form, with a host of extra equipment.

Due to the good offices of my friend John Norwood in New York, the public relations branch of Studebaker-Packard arranged to lend George Phillips and me one of the latest Daytona machines, equipped with everything bar the kitchen stove. Stirling Moss also had a Lark, but his had automatic transmission, not fitted to any of the really hot versions.

"Our" car was brought, appropriately enough, from Daytona Beach, by local dealer Fred Chase, and delivered to Sebring race H.Q. It was finished in Alfa Romeo red, with black-and-white upholstery. Fred pointed out that it was not exactly a stock model, as it had four-speed, all synchromesh gearbox with "stick-shift", extra large turbo brakes with vacuum-servo operation to the twin master cylinders, powered steering, twin-traction drive, full air-conditioning, sunshine roof, extra-comfort Reutter-pattern front seats, dual exhaust system and stiffened rear suspension. As regards the power unit, this was a tuned version of the 4.2-litre V8, with "four-barrel" carburetter. He mentioned, in passing, that one could also have the 4.7-litre engine from the Hawk, but added that the "small motor" was every bit as good.

Quite candidly this was a surprising car in every way, and if it had any vices, neither Phil nor I discovered them. Also very impressed was racing driver Peter Bolton, who said that it was streets ahead of any American car that he had ever tried. There are many twisty roads around Sebring and also several with switchback characteristics which soon find out roadability, or rather the lack of it. The Daytona Lark was perfectly at home; there were no signs of pitching and tossing or tail-happiness, even when the car was being driven like a sports model. Potential performance was immense, and it was only the thought of languishing in the sheriff's caboose, or forking out plenty of iron men, that prevented us from discovering the ultimate performance.

Nevertheless, on one or two occasions we rushed up to 110 m.p.h. with the big V8 engine turning over like a turbine, and apparently asking for more. Engine silence was uncanny, although there was quite a healthy boom from the tail-pipes.

It was difficult to realize that powered steering was fitted, for the car had none of the "deadness" often found with assisted direction. In fact, the steering was first-class, although both of us would have preferred a lower ratio. Braking was remarkably good and there is little doubt that the outsize drums,

with their heavy finning, are well up to the car's performance. Discs are talked about, of course, and I believe that it is only a matter of time before Studebaker introduce them on their passenger cars.

We had nothing but praise for the gearbox, which, to give it the highest possible praise, is as efficient as anything produced by Porsche or Volvo. The ratios are well chosen, which encourages one to use the box to its fullest extent, despite the fact that the top-gear performance is most impressive. It is possible to tool along at about 10 m.p.h. in top, without the slightest sign of

ABOVE: OFFICE: Simple and effective treatment of the facia panel on the Daytona Lark. Lever for the four-speed gearbox is below the air-conditioning control unit. Anti-crash padding is featured.

BELOW: POWER-PACKED: The V8 engine occupies practically the entire bonnet space. Instrument on left is not a supercharger, but the air-conditioning and refrigerating motor.

snatch and then bang down the pedal to the floorboards, when the car immediately responds.

Gear ratios were 7.28, 5.49, 4.34 and 3.31 to 1, the box being almost identical to that used on G.M.'s Corvette. Maximum speeds in gears were: 1st, 55 m.p.h.; 2nd, 75 m.p.h.; and 3rd, 90 m.p.h. At none of these speeds was valve-crash evident: the engine just ran out of revs. No tachometer was fitted, but calculation shows that at 55 m.p.h. in low gear the V8 was turning over at above 5,000 r.p.m.

The suspension was not stiffened up as much as were the modified Larks which ran in a saloon car race at Sebring a couple of years back and therefore the

ride at all times was good. Another excellent point was the absolute impossibility to provoke rear-wheel tramp, not always absent on American cars fitted with lusty V8 power units.

Whilst the general finish is of a high standard, I deplored the imitation walnut-finish on the facia. It tends to spoil what is otherwise a handsome panel and ought to be replaced. The rear boot lid does not remain in an open position and one is apt to receive a nasty crack on the head unless one is exceptionally careful. Again, it is necessary to lock the lid otherwise it will not

close. These are just two items that might annoy potential buyers.

The car did not appear to be unduly heavy on petrol and I would put consumption at around 20 m.p. U.S. gallon, driving rather harder than one ought to with so many coppers about. Starting was always instantaneous, but there was a tendency for the engine to stall in traffic.

We handed back the Daytona with great reluctance. It had shown both of us that American automobile engineers can turn out a vehicle which is equally suited to the give-and-take roads of Europe, as well as the effortless cruising which makes motoring with large-engined cars such a delight.

STUDEBAKER

Add stronger anchors to this flagship of the Studebaker fleet and you'd have a dreamboat

STUDEBAKER's Gran Turismo Hawk left us with truly mixed feelings. In some ways, it was the most appealing car we've driven this year. Yet, on one vital point, it was among the most disappointing.

In accord with our usual test procedure, we pushed the Hawk to 80 mph and hit the brake pedal. The brakes grabbed efficiently, slowing the car in a straight, even line. Smoothly, swiftly, we dropped to about 20 mph—but, at that speed, all braking effect was gone! The linings had completely faded. Fortunately, we had enough road left to coast to a stop.

We believe this was a peculiar weakness of our test vehicle and wouldn't occur, at least to such a serious degree, with most other examples of the marque. Still, we can't justify *any* car losing its brakes so thoroughly during a single fast stop. Normal wear and tear isn't an excuse; our car had less than 5000 miles on its odometer.

The Hawk has the same standard brakes as the Lark V-8, though with finned drums. On the surface, this seems reasonable because the bigger car isn't significantly heavier. Our Hawk, in fact, weighed the same as the Lark V-8 Daytona convertible we discussed in last month's issue.

However, the two cars differ in purpose. The Hawk invites much harder, faster driving than its compact running mate. It's a brisk, roadable machine and ought to be able to stop, we think, as well as it goes.

To its credit, Studebaker offers an option that should improve matters, heavy-duty, oversize brakes providing a 23-sq. in. increase in lining area. We earnestly recommend these to any motorist who wants a Hawk for something more than an ornament in his driveway.

That ends our major criticism of the Gran Turismo Hawk. In most other respects, it's very much the kind of car we'd be happy to own.

The styling, for example, drew compliments wherever we went. The basic body shell dates back to the 1953 Studebaker coupe created by Raymond Loewy—the re-design for 1962 is the work of Brooks Stevens. Highlighting the new look is a simple, squared-off roof line which is said to derive from the Packard Predictor, an experimental car built six years ago by Studebaker's silenced partner. It looks pure Thunderbird to us, though. Somebody is apparently engaging in a little double-think in anticipation of the 1984 model!

The interior is just as handsome as the exterior. For the man who really enjoys driving, the Hawk has one of the most attractive and functional cockpits of any automobile built in this country. That statement covers not only such obvious things as the complete set of legible instruments, including an optional tachometer, but subtleties like the forward placement of the steering wheel and the careful arrangement of the brake and accelerator pedals to permit heel-and-toeing.

We found it most refreshing to sit behind a panel of gauges that told us what was really happening under the hood, instead of relaying vague bits of information through flashing lights. In addition, the dash features toggle switches for minor controls, eliminating the mystery of whether to push, pull or twist.

The front bucket seats are high from the floor and, with a simple fore-and-aft adjustment, provide a wider range of genuine comfort than some 6-way power seats. Both the shortest and tallest of our staffers were able to find excellent driving positions.

There are a couple of interior refinements for 1962 that we particularly appreciated. The ash tray has been moved from the door panel to a much more accessible spot in a new console between the front seats, while the parking brake handle has been re-positioned to avoid tangling with the 4-speed floor shift lever.

Our car was powered by the 289-cu.-in. Studebaker V-8, developing 225 bhp with an optional 4-barrel carburetor. The standard version has 210 bhp with a 2-barrel. Both engines have 8.5:1 compression ratios to allow the use of regular fuel, down slightly from last year's 8.8:1.

▶

Gran Turismo Hawk

PHOTOS BY MARVIN LYONS

Gran Turismo Hawk
continued

Because the Hawk is something of an enthusiast's car, the optional 4-speed gearbox would seem to be an appropriate item of equipment. Actually, this particular installation is more for fun than function. The Studebaker engine is flexible enough that it doesn't really need 4 closely-grouped gears. In traffic, we sometimes found ourselves shifting from 1st to 4th, skipping the intermediate ratios.

Still, the smooth shifting action with the floor lever does add to driving enjoyment and, on that basis, the 4-speed can be justified. The unit is, of course, the familiar Warner box with the "big car" ratios, 2.54:1 in 1st, 1.92 in 2nd and 1.51 in 3rd. Because of the Hawk's engine characteristics, closer gears than these would serve little purpose.

Other transmissions available are a standard 3-speed with a 2.57:1 first gear and 1.55 second, and the Borg-Warner automatic described in last month's report on the Daytona.

The 3-speed can also be fitted with overdrive, a combination that strikes us as the most practical of all for the Hawk. It provides the broadest range of gearing, allowing the use of a strong rear axle ratio without sacrificing highway economy. With a 3.73 axle, the 3-speed has over-all gearing of 9.59:1 in 1st, 5.78 in 2nd, 4.05 in 2nd overdrive, 3.73 in 3rd and 2.61 in 3rd overdrive. By way of comparison, the same axle with 4-speed provides 9.48:1 in 1st, 7.09 in 2nd, 5.63 in 3rd and, of course, 3.73 in 4th. Obviously, the overdrive is more

versatile, though we'll admit the 3-speed's column lever isn't nearly as entertaining as the 4-speed's floor shift!

The final element in the Hawk's sporting appeal is road-worthy suspension, providing a smooth, stable feel under most normal conditions. Beyond 70 mph, the floating tendencies become a little discomfiting but those who spend much time at high speeds can correct the problem with export springs and shock absorbers.

Cornering ability is surprisingly good, considering the car's front-end weight bias and long, 120.5-in. wheelbase. The nose plows somewhat in tight turns but body sway is moderate and traction secure. When the rear wheels finally break loose, they do so gradually enough that the driver has plenty of time to correct.

While the Hawk isn't as exciting as a 400-cu. in. Super Stock, it's a lot easier to live with. It's a companionable sort of car that doesn't require much effort in traffic, yet responds to considerable driving verve on the open road. ■

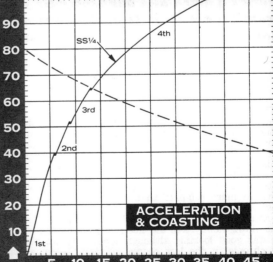

CAR LIFE ROAD TEST

GranTurismo

STUDEBAKER HAWK

SPECIFICATIONS

List price	$3095
Price, as tested	3788
Curb weight, lb	3530
Test weight	3835
distribution, %	56.2/43.8
Tire size	6.70-15
Tire capacity, lb	3680
Brake swept area	282
Engine type	V-8, ohv
Bore & stroke	3.56 x 3.62
Displacement, cu in	289
Compression ratio	8.5
Bhp @ rpm	225 @ 4500
equivalent mph	96.1
Torque, lb-ft	305 @ 3000
equivalent mph	64.1

EXTRA-COST OPTIONS

225-bhp engine, 4-speed transmission, limited slip differential, power brakes, power steering, wsw tires, tachometer, radio, heater, reclining front seats, safety belts.

DIMENSIONS

Wheelbase, in	120.5
Tread, f and r	57.4/56.6
Over-all length, in	204
width	71.0
height	54.7
equivalent vol, cu ft	459
Frontal area, sq ft	21.6
Ground clearance, in	7.5
Steering ratio, o/a	24.5
turns, lock to lock	4.6
turning circle, ft	42.5
Hip room, front	2 x 21.8
Hip room, rear	58.0
Pedal to seat back, max	42.0
Floor to ground	12.0
Luggage vol, cu ft	n.a.
Fuel tank capacity, gal	18.0

GEAR RATIOS

4th (1.00), overall		3.73
3rd (1.51)		5.63
2nd (1.92)		7.16
1st (2.54)		9.48

PERFORMANCE

Top speed (5000), mph	103
best timed run	n.a.
3rd (5000)	70
2nd (5000)	55
1st (5000)	42

ACCELERATION

0-30 mph, sec	4.2
0-40	6.3
0-50	8.5
0-60	11.4
0-70	15.7
0-80	21.0
0-100	38.0
Standing ¼ mile	18.2
speed at end	75

FUEL CONSUMPTION

Normal range, mpg	14-18

SPEEDOMETER ERROR

30 mph, actual	28.9
60 mph	55.8
90 mph	84.0

CALCULATED DATA

Lb/hp (test wt)	17.0
Cu ft/ton mile	122.5
Mph/1000 rpm	21.4
Engine revs/mile	2810
Piston travel, ft/mile	1700
Car Life wear index	47.7

PULLING POWER

4th, lb/ton @ mph	240 @ 58
3rd	390 @ 49
2nd	480 @ 43
Total drag at 60 mph, lb	145

ACCELERATION & COASTING

SS¼

4th

3rd

2nd

1st

MPH — ELAPSED TIME IN SECONDS — 5 10 15 20 25 30 35 40 45

Studebaker GT has a bold front that is not too ornate. Radiator grille is decidedly Studebaker.

STUDEBAKER
Genuine American GT

Here's a quick and handsome GT car from Studebaker. It goes, stops and handles — and is not too costly.

By PETER HALL

THE Golden and Silver Hawks of recent years have been logical developments of the famous classic Studebaker coupe of 1953 — the last car Raymond Loewy designed for the firm until the sensational, and quite radical, Avanti came off the drawing boards this year. The 1953 Stude, a truly beautiful car, was a sales flop and contributed much to the company's later decision to bring out the compact Lark (which was no more compact than the '53 itself) to solve mid-50's financial troubles.

Apart from the supercharged Golden Hawk of 1957, the Hawk family tree did not really shake the earth. It was good looking, although tending to an obesity of chrome in the last couple of years — somewhat of a compromise between the sporting machinery it looked and the fast American-style basic transport it was used for by most who bought it.

But when the Gran Turismo model was released as America's only "genuine" Grand Touring car of 1962, the pattern seemed to change.

For a start, the Hawk was given the full Continental treatment as far as body styling was concerned and a full range of power and transmission options gave it a lot of performance potential.

Because the GT is being assembled here in the small volume obviously all our market can take of this rather specialised and pricy machine, there is only one basic model, sharing its mechanical specifications with last year's Silver Hawk and a lot of components with the bread-and-butter Lark V8.

In spite of Studebaker's growing volume of Australian sales, the new model Hawk has been given a price rise of £102, making it £2397, including sales tax.

Apart from the obvious changes in the bodywork, such as the flat back window and "Thunderbird" type quarter panels at the back, the new Hawk is improved in many ways.

WHEELS FULL ROAD TEST

Doors are wide and absence of floor wells makes for easy and complete cleaning inside the car. Seat is a bench, would be better as two buckets.

Actually, the new roofline and back window arrangement is not pure decoration. They allow much more space in the back seat for two, even occasionally three, people, and the driver's vision is much improved.

Older Hawks lacked headroom in the back seat and the seating space itself was cramped too close to the divided front seats.

The tiny side vent windows at the back of the old Hawk have been replaced by generous wind-down panes that vanish into the bodywork. The side pillar is gone so that the GT is a hardtop coupe that gives an uninterrupted flow of air and a sense of being sporty on those days when the occupants are game enough to wind down all the windows.

The dashboard has been completely redesigned and is now fitted with a more comprehensive set of instruments than is, or has been fitted to, any other American car I can think of.

In front of the driver is a vast steel panel, tinted to look like wood, with no fewer than seven dials.

On his left is a big VDO electric rev counter—of more use on a standard transmission model than on the automatic available here. On the far right is a big electric clock that kept perfect time in the three days I had the car.

In the main panel right in front of the driver are a very optimistic speedo (11 mph fast at top speed), fuel gauge, oil pressure gauge, water temperature gauge and ammeter. All the dials were black with white pointers and markings.

At night, a variable white light illuminated the dials as well as the ignition keyhole and recess for the cigarette lighter.

The only unfortunate part of this excellent instrument layout is a ghastly speckled black and white fibreglass pressing surrounding it. The rest of the

Dashboard is very well instrumented, even includes a tachometer and unusually reliable clock. Powerful heater is standard equipment.

Engine is a moderate-sized V8, by American standards, but it develops enough power to push the car along at well over the 100 mph mark.

dashboard looks a bit cheap, too, although it is actually a quite respectable slab of spun aluminium. A roomy glovebox in front of the passenger and safety padding covered the top of the dash.

Seating is of better quality and more comfortable than last year, but the arrangement in the front is an unnecessary compromise. It consists of a single seat with two separate squabs.

A high transmission tunnel made the carriage of a third person in the front highly unlikely for distance motoring and there seems little reason, unless it was cost, why the Australian GT should not have followed the American model pattern and been fitted with genuine separate bucket seats.

The seats themselves are deeply padded, well shaped and covered in good quality vinyl colored in irridescent tones. The squabs of the front seats fold well forward so that, with the exceptionally wide opening provided by the broad doors, access to the back seat is quite easy.

Ashtrays are one of the weakest points in the Studebaker GT. The driver's is fitted to the front door as close to the dashboard as possible. It only has a narrow opening, so that the smoking driver tends to deposit ash all over the thick carpet, instead of in the tray.

Ash on the carpet is not as annoying as it sounds, really. The GT shares with its cheaper Lark brothers one outstanding feature—the floors are flush with what is left of the running board. There is no deep well to pick dust, bits of paper and cigarette butts—you just flick everything straight out with a brush.

One of the technical improvements on the GT Hawk is the fitting of power brakes. The unit used is Australia's own VH24, by PBR: Braking power was one of the former Hawk's strong points, and the power assistance has made it even better. Unlike most American cars of the Hawk's power, fade is very hard to induce. You can get it, of course, probably partly because the car is fitted with big chromed wheel discs that effectively strangle cooling draughts of air trying to get through the wheel slots.

Although no suspension modifications are listed, the GT seemed to handle better than the former model. The steering (six turns from lock to lock) is still unnecessarily low-geared and the turning circle (45 ft) too broad, but at least the front-heavy Hawk is easy to turn at low speeds.

You have to do a lot of winding when you try to treat it as you would better known and more genuine GT machinery from other countries, but high speed touring on reasonably good roads is sheer pleasure.

The GT Hawk understeers gracefully, its big 15 in wheels give it a sure grip and the suspension seems almost as hard as an MG TC. Indeed, on rough roads, you get quite a shaking in this he-man's car.

Power is in the king-size class. The ohv 4.7 litre V8 engine churns out a hefty 225 bhp that throbs pleasantly away in the distance at a scorching rate of knots through the big twin exhaust system.

A simple Borg-Warner three-speed automatic transmission is fitted, but the Stude is still capable of hair-raising acceleration times and a top speed around 110 mph—probably more given perfect tune, the right road and sufficient room.

This well-proven transmission is pretty efficient on the GT. Under full power, the changes of ratio are rather violent, but instantaneous, which is how they should be in a GT car, if they must be fitted with automatic gears.

Around the city, the Hawk GT is a delight. Apart from the ego-pleasing looks, the shattering acceleration at traffic lights and the sheer comfort, driving is quite effortless.

Out on the open road and in challenging country, one tends to yearn for the optional floor change, four-speed transmission that is available in the United States.

Actually, Hawk GT lovers can get such a car, but it would have to be fully imported and would cost around £2900.

And they would not get the excellent heater that is thrown in as standard equipment on the Australian-produced model.

My last comment on the car is one tinged with sheer relief and joy. For the last couple of years the Hawk has been despoiled by hidious tail fins.

Now, they have gone — completely and, I hope, forever. Thus. The Hawk GT has virtually no challenger to the title of best looking American car available here.   #

Roof line is handsome and provides ample room inside for backseat passengers. Side windows can be wound all the way down into body.

wheels ROAD TEST

TECHNICAL DETAILS

OF THE

STUDEBAKER HAWK GT

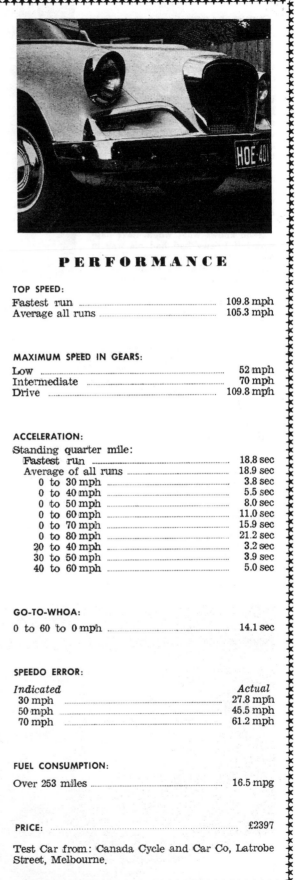

SPECIFICATIONS

ENGINE:

Cylinders	8, vee formation
Bore and Stroke	90.4 by 91.8 mm
Cubic capacity	4737 cc (289 cu in)
Compression ratio	7.5 to 1
Valves	pushrod, overhead
Carburettor	four barrel
Power at rpm	225 at 4500 rpm
Max torque	310 lb ft at 2800 rpm

TRANSMISSION:

Type	Automatic

SUSPENSION:

Front	Independent, coil springs
Back	Semi-elliptic leaf springs
Shockers	Telescopic

STEERING:

Type	cam and lever
Turns, 1 to 1	6¼
Turning circle	45 ft

BRAKES:

Type	drum, power assisted

DIMENSIONS:

Wheelbase	10 ft 0½ in
Track, front	4 ft 9¾ in
Track, rear	4 ft 11⅛ in
Length	17 ft
Width	5 ft 11.3 in
Height	4 ft 7 in (loaded)

TYRES:

Size	6.70 by 15

WEIGHT:

Kerb	28¾ cwt

PERFORMANCE

TOP SPEED:

Fastest run	109.8 mph
Average all runs	105.3 mph

MAXIMUM SPEED IN GEARS:

Low	52 mph
Intermediate	70 mph
Drive	109.8 mph

ACCELERATION:

Standing quarter mile:

Fastest run	18.8 sec
Average of all runs	18.9 sec
0 to 30 mph	3.8 sec
0 to 40 mph	5.5 sec
0 to 50 mph	8.0 sec
0 to 60 mph	11.0 sec
0 to 70 mph	15.9 sec
0 to 80 mph	21.2 sec
20 to 40 mph	3.2 sec
30 to 50 mph	3.9 sec
40 to 60 mph	5.0 sec

GO-TO-WHOA:

0 to 60 to 0 mph	14.1 sec

SPEEDO ERROR:

Indicated	Actual
30 mph	27.8 mph
50 mph	45.5 mph
70 mph	61.2 mph

FUEL CONSUMPTION:

Over 253 miles	16.5 mpg

PRICE: £2397

Test Car from: Canada Cycle and Car Co, Latrobe Street, Melbourne.

STUDEBAKER have had the itch to be different from America's Big Three ever since Raymond Loewy designed for them the very successful "which-way-is-it-going?" look back in 1947.

That sparked off a revolution in U.S. body styling. Then, in 1953, Loewy produced for them the first of the Hawk coupe designs. This, too, was a success—the 1962 Gran Turismo Hawk still follows the same basic concept.

But Studebaker hadn't the courage to accept Loewy's 1953 designs for their bread-and-butter cars. There was very little of either bread or butter for the company until it thought up the Lark.

Who knows what would have happened if Loewy had had his way in 1953? No one, of course. But the fact remains that his coupe concept has been in production almost ten years.

The current model has been shorn of the hideous fins which Studebaker

THE ADVANCED

grafted on, and which kept growing right up 'till last year. A general tidying-up has turned it into one of the most attractive American cars yet put on the road—and it has far more than just styling.

Interior, Equipment

The Hawk is neither a true G.T. machine nor a sports car. But it has both the looks and the performance to put it in a very select class.

It is a true coupe, with only two doors. Yet inside there is plenty of room for six people. Apart from the lowness of the body, the doors are wide enough for them to fall in and out, back or front.

The seats are superb — deeply upholstered but firm. Covering is that grade of plastic that looks far more like leather than anything any animal has yet produced.

I would have liked to see bucket seats in front instead of the bench with split, fold-forward squabs. The bench has ample width for a central

passenger—but the big transmission hump forces him to sit slightly side-saddle.

The floor is covered with something that just passes muster as carpet. Headlining is plastic. The back seat has two fixed armrests and two ashtrays. There are coathooks on the roof at each side, and a single central roof light that works off the doors or off the main lights switch on the dash. Nothing very Gran Turismo yet.

The driver is the boy who gets the

DRIVER gets fully-adjustable seat, well-placed controls, every instrument, including a rev-counter.

LONG, heavy bonnet hides massive single-camshaft, 225 b.h.p. V8, coupled to a Borg-Warner automatic.

Studebaker Hawk G.T. offers a stylish coupe body with room for six, 107 m.p.h. performance and roadholding to match, reports Bryan Hanrahan

ate — neat white markings on matt-black dials.

Dash padding is adequate rather than overdone. The whole assembly is matt-black — except for some cheap-looking tin dressed up to look like tea-chest plywood.

Electric two-speed screen-wipers, powerful pump-action screen-washers, an electric clock and a cigarette lighter round off the dash equipment.

Handbrake is one of those twist-and-pull arrangements that give you a fine sense of insecurity, no matter how hard you pull. But that's not its worst point—it's located immediately below an unpadded edge of the dash. As you let it off, it tends to trap your fingers.

P N D L R, without even an intermediate-gear hold. Control is by steering-column quadrant and accelerator kickdown.

Action, though, was very smooth— as you'd expect with nearly five litres of engine capacity and 225 horses to play with. It was responsive quickly to kickdown and only intruded into smooth progress when changing up under full throttle. Whined a bit in low gear.

If you don't kick down, the car starts in second gear.

G.T.-plus Performance

I wonder if we'll ever see in Australia the fantastic ranges of options that are offered in the States with so many popular models—alternative engines, axle ratios and transmissions. This could be a highly rewarding car with four-speed gearbox and a lever on the floor. Even one of the new "non-automatic" automatics, with which you can override practically every involuntary function, would be nice.

There's no doubt about performance. The big, single-camshaft V8, breathing through a twin-choke downdraught carby, puts out its best at 4500 r.p.m. on a compression ratio of 8.25 to 1. Like most of these massive American units, it was quiet right up to peak revs and never, never fussy.

Full kickdown treatment produced 55 m.p.h. in first, 70 in second. Top speed over the flying quarter-mile averaged out at 107.2 m.p.h., with

AMERICAN

full treatment. A wheel that DOESN'T poke into his face or chest. Bags of seat adjustment. And a battery of well-placed instruments instead of warning lights — rev-counter, speedometer (regrettably without a trip recorder), genuine gauges for water temperature, oil pressure, ammeter and fuel-tank contents.

True, this is the minimum by G.T. standards—but whoever heard of any popular American with even half this array? And the Hawk's dials are legible, finely calibrated and accur-

Window-winders are badly placed and slow in action. But the back quarter-lights pivot down flush with the sills, so that the whole of each side can be opened. Very pleasant in the right weather, in true coupe style.

Finish, taken all·round, is pretty good—as it seems to be with most Americans assembled here. They certainly show up the imported ones of a few years back!

Transmission is very plain three-speed Borg Warner. The usual

MPLE room for three in comfortably upholstered rear seat. All side windows drop down out of sight.

BOOT is vast, despite the spare wheel, and neatly finished; but lifting lid is almost a two-man job.

COMING or going?—A distinctive feature of Studebaker Hawk is the dummy grille on boot lid. Twin exhausts hide under a hefty bumper.

a best one-way run of 111.5. The standing quarter was swallowed up in 18.7 seconds. Eighty came up from rest in less than 20 seconds. That's Gran Turismo style—and then some.

Was I pleased to see that tubeless tyres were NOT fitted to a car with this sort of performance! Canada Cycle and Motor Company, who assemble Studebakers in Victoria, seem to be the only people who have taken notice of the fact that tubeless tyres are banned on racetracks — and rightly so, since this Hawk is thoroughly capable of being operated at racing speeds.

You might not know that the popular types of tyres produced in Australia are not recommended by the makers for running at sustained speeds above 90 m.p.h. A sobering thought with a really fast car.

Handling, Brakes

Suspension and brakes are unique in my experience of American machinery.

Front end is a development of the MacPherson system—combined coil-spring and shocker struts on each side, mounted high up in the wings. An anti-roll bar ties the independent action together. At the back, conventional semi-elliptics are damped by telescopic shockers.

The ride is distinctly firm at low speeds. Cruising, it smooths out to a completely painless degree. On the corners you get the benefit: she sits down like a well-licked postage stamp.

The Hawk understeers, but nowhere near to the point that some of its contemporaries do—I mean the point of no return.

If the steering weren't so hopelessly undergeared at five turns lock-to-lock, this would be a very handy package for its all-up weight of 1½ tons on test. The steering does redeem itself a bit by transmitting the feel of the road. Not enough, though. And it's still rather heavy at low speeds.

Braking is contrived with the help of big finned drums on the front wheels. A power unit took all the muscle work out of working them. They pulled up straight after several good hammerings. They did NOT fade to any degree worth reporting. Again something unique in my dealings with the big Americans.

The price of this performance on test was 17.2 m.p.g.

Oddly enough, the clumsier features of the car were concerned mainly with the beautiful body shell. The great snout of a bonnet is almost a two-man lift, even though it has a system of spring assistance. Must have been designed for springing mousetraps. Only an outside catch, too.

The two wide doors have the inside hardware set in awkward spots. They, too, are extremely heavy to open and close.

Boot is of the "lean over and dive in" type, long and shallow. Spare is tucked away nicely to one side.

The turning circle of 44ft. 2in. (between walls) doesn't make parking a pleasure.

The other out-of-keeping feature was the heater-demister — a recirculatory type, on a car costing £2397 tax-paid.

Quite a shock, I got. These things not only work on the stale air in the car—they need the fan on all the time. And the fan was indecently noisy at any useful speed in the stillness of the Stude.

There's enough space under the bonnet to fit three or four fresh-air heaters. Why not use it? A few more quid on the price wouldn't be noticed by people who buy in this rarefied class.

But if this Studebaker isn't entirely Gran Turismo, it's all motor-car, in the best sense of the term. The most advanced American by far that I've driven.

● ● ●

MAIN SPECIFICATIONS

ENGINE: V8, o.h.v., single camshaft; bore 3.56in., stroke 3.63in., capacity 289cu. ih. (4737c.c.); compression ratio 8.25:1; maximum b.h.p. 225 at 4500 r.p.m.; maximum torque 300lb./ft. at 2800 r.p.m.; twin-choke downdraught carburettor, mechanical fuel pump; 12v. ignition.
TRANSMISSION: Borg-Warner, three-speed automatic.
SUSPENSION: Front independent, by MacPherson-strut system and anti-roll bar; semi-elliptics at rear; telescopic hydraulic shock-absorbers all round.

STEERING: Cam-and-lever; 5 turns lock-to-lock, 44ft. 2in. turning circle.
WHEELS: Pressed-steel discs, with 6.70 by 15in. tyres.
BRAKES: Hydraulic, 172.8 sq. in. lining area.
DIMENSIONS: Wheelbase, 10ft. 0½in.; track, front 4ft. 9 3-8in., rear 4ft. 8½in., length 17ft., width 5ft. 11¾in., height 4ft. 7in.; ground clearance 7½in.
KERB WEIGHT: 28¾cwt.
FUEL TANK: 15 gallons.

PERFORMANCE ON TEST

CONDITIONS: Fine, warm; no wind; smooth bitumen; two occupants, premium fuel.
BEST SPEED: 111.5 m.p.h.
FLYING quarter-mile: 107.2 m.p.h.
STANDING quarter-mile: 18.7s.
MAXIMUM in indirect gears: 1st, 55 m.p.h.; 2nd, 70.
ACCELERATION from rest through gears (using fixed Low and full kick-down): 0-30, 3.8s.; 0-40, 5.6s.; 0-50, 7.8s.; 0-60, 9.9s.; 0-70, 14.0s.;

0-80, 19.7s.; 0-90, 25.2s.; 0-100, 37.6s.
PASSING ACCELERATION in Drive range (using full kick-down): 20-40, 3.1s.; 30-50, 4.2s.; 40-60, 4.8s.; 50-70, 7.0s.; 60-80, 10.2s.; 70-90, 13.4s.; 80-100, 18.9s.
BRAKING: 32ft. 11in. to stop from 30 m.p.h. in neutral.
FUEL CONSUMPTION: 17.2 m.p.g. overall for 210-mile test.
SPEEDO: Accurate at 30 m.p.h.; 3 m.p.h. fast at 90.

PRICE: £2397 including tax

130 mph
132 mph

138 mph
140 mph

Two New Cars are Born

Avanti-inspired...
Bonneville-tested!

R2 SUPER LARK
R2 SUPER HAWK

We designed two new cars—and built a lot of our record-setting Avanti into them. Added the supercharged Avanti R2 engine.

...And took them to the Flats for final evaluation and endurance tests. The results surprised even us: R2 Super Lark—132 mph! R2 Super Hawk—140 mph! With 2 up. Under bad weather and surface conditions—even snow. USAC timed the bit, official.

That kind of performance told us these cars were ready to join the Studebaker line. R2 Super Lark and R2 Super Hawk are now available on special order at your Studebaker dealer's.

The package of pow and pizazz:
R-2 blown mill, 4-speed box, Avanti wheels inside 6.50-15's. Anti-sway rod forward; trac rods, rear. HD springs and shocks at both ends. Our disc binders. Belts. (Now installed on **all**

cars from Studebaker, by the way.) Sundry little signs on each car to tell the peasantry you've got an extreme automobile. When parked. Under way, they'll know without sign language. Warning: The color choice is limited. But you have your own spray gun, don't you?

Studebaker
C O R P O R A T I O N

Refinements to Australia's cheapest V8 have made it a better car than before.

BY

PETER

HALL

LARK'S TRIM NEW

Rear end styling is rather complex, could easily be mistaken for the front from some angles.

WITH the throb of V8 engines and the occasional screech of Victorian Police sirens, Studebaker is becoming a motoring power in the land.

After a decade in which the total number of Studebakers sold per year in Australia could be counted by the dunce of a kindergarten arithmetic class, the make started a swift climb back to volume in 1960.

With restrictions on the import of dollar goods lifted almost completely, a few fully-imported Studebakers appeared on showroom floors.

They did not sell very well—they cost well over £2000 and even the most rabid Studebaker fan had to admit they were rather ugly comfortless machines, reflecting the corporate difficulties the parent manufacturer was having in America.

But the old-established Melbourne distributor, Canada Cycle and Car Company, which had built its fortunes on Dodge in the old days, took the Victorian franchise and, much more importantly, the Australian concession to assemble the Studebaker range at the small factory it had in the Melbourne suburb of Tottenham, for the national market.

The project began slowly but surely, especially when the credit squeeze descended on the car industry like a great dark cloud, and there were many frowns on the brows of Canada Cycle executives.

Left: Exterior treatment of the Lark is a little more fussy than before but appearance is generally improved.

Below: The interior of the Lark is quite neat and well laid out. Lap straps are standard in the front.

FEATHERS

But in 1961 the project started to get properly in its stride. Studebakers had great success in events like the Armstrong 500 and the Victorian police decided to switch its fast highway fleet from Fords to Studebakers.

The public sat up and took notice. It also bought about 600 Studebakers that year.

In 1962, a better looking range of sedans and the Hawk coupe were released, and the salesmen found they had a solid niche in the Australian big car market.

Indeed, it was a solid niche, as the sales figures for 1962 showed. Nearly 1100 Studebakers were sold for the year. The make had more than 10 percent of the big car field and had come from nowhere to fifth place behind Ford Fairlane, Chevrolet, Humber and Mercedes-Benz.

This year, Canada Cycle has expanded its production facilities and sales are going well enough to take Studebaker past both Humber and Mercedes-Benz and land the make right on the tail of the big two in the Australian luxury car field.

A very creditable effort indeed, particularly in view of the fact that the Studebaker people, do not possess a dealer organisation nearly as big and solidly entrenched as either Ford's or Chevrolet's.

What has put Studebaker so quickly into the Australian big car fight?

Sampling the latest versions of the main seller—the Lark sedan—I have concluded there are several very understandable reasons.

The first, I think, is the name. For several decades, a large number of middle and upper class Australians have known and respected the Studebaker name. The public at large, too, views the name favorably, if only because it remembers that it was Studebaker who set the pace in postwar car design with the first coming-or-going car in 1947—and probably made the best looking of all the back-to-front models.

(In Victoria, there is another special reason—southerners are always catching glimpses of their traffic police tearing about in powder-blue Studebakers).

But another, much more important reason, is that the new model, as in the last two years, is exceptionally good motoring value.

In keeping with a policy proved by firms like Ford, Volkswagen and Peugeot, the Studebaker is not greatly changed for 1963.

But the changes that have been made, with one arguable exception, have all been very much worthwhile.

The appearance, to start with, has been altered

sufficiently to remove just about all the early Studebaker Lark's chunkiness.

Last year, the maker switched to a protruding, lattice-work radiator grille reminiscent of the famous Mercedes-Benz grille. This year, the grille has been smoothed and the accent placed on the horizontal bars of the smaller squares, to give an impression that the car is lower.

The profile of the basically similar car (wheelbase and overall length are exactly the same) has been "lifted" to make the Lark look longer and a little flightier.

The wraparound edges of the windscreen have gone and the screen is flatter and its pillars neater. Door edges have been squared and a quarter light that, unfortunately, does not open, is fitted to the back door.

The quarter panel of metal behind the back door is heavier and five little slicks of chrome fixed to it to break up the "Fordish" look.

A neat waistline of chrome is now fitted that flares out to an attractive panel of aluminium.

Much work was done to the dumpy tail end of last year. This time, the back is merely decorated, with more beaten aluminium and bigger amber turn lights.

Of great benefit at night is the wiring arrangement whereby the amber lights automatically double as backing lights when the driver selects reverse gear.

Inside, there are more changes including the one that is of arguable use.

Called an "Exclusive Beauty Vanity" in the sales' blurb, it is a rather complicated box arrangement that takes the place of the conventional glove box.

In it are three boxes for storing mylady's cosmetics and a collapsable mirror that sits up at an angle when the contraption is opened.

Apparently Studebaker's market researchers found that the ladies were never madly enthusiastic about using mirrors behind the passenger's sun visor—the angle is an unflattering one.

So, the designers hit on this vanity case idea which seems to me, a mere man, an utter waste of space. If the ladies stuff their lipsticks and powders and what-have-you in the little compartments, the man of the car has no hope of doing anything with his pipe, or spare packet of tranquillisers or ever-useful spanner.

The whole thing is actually tied up with the insidious idea that it is really the women who choose the new cars these days.

But for the rest of the interior, the alterations to the Studebaker Lark are good ones.

The seats, well shaped last year, are better this year, although the new, soft vinyl trim is colored rather garishly for my taste.

The door trim is now carried right up to the window sills, in the current and excellent American fashion.

The dashboard and instrument layout has been redesigned and has thicker safety padding fixed on the top and bottom edges.

The instruments and controls are still grouped directly in front of the driver. But a large binnacle now surrounds them, effectively eliminating reflections in the windscreen and large white buttons are now used to operate windscreen wipers, lights and so on.

Studebaker has dropped last year's scruffy imitation wood/tin dash panel and substituted more honest (and more handsome) aluminium.

A large, half-circle horn ring is fitted in place of the narrow, hard-to-reach button that stretched across the two wheel spokes last year.

A wholly admirable switch this year is to two-speed electric windscreen wipers. Also, the makers have dropped the separate arc arrangement with its large unswept area of glass in the centre, in favor of parallel sweeping wipers.

But here, Studebaker has made an error common to American cars assembled in Australia—the wipers use the same pivot points as on the original left-hand drive cars.

Result is an annoying patch of unswept glass in the top right hand corner of the windscreen. This would not be so annoying if the driver's seat was not so high and upright—a medium size fellow myself, I nevertheless looked straight through the unswept portion of the screen.

In line with the American parent company's new 1963 policy, all the '63 Studes sold here are fitted with lap-type seat belts in the front as standard equipment.

If you don't like seat belts, you can order them removed and doubtless enjoy a slight reduction in the price of the car.

Other equipment includes windscreen washers, cigarette lighter, useless but allegedly decorative trim rings on the wheels, and an internal bonnet lock.

The automatic model, which sells for an extra £161, also has a heater and demister.

CONTINUED ON PAGE 68

Humble glovebox has been converted into a vanity drawer for lady passengers.

wheels ROAD TEST

TECHNICAL DETAILS
STUDEBAKER LARK
1963

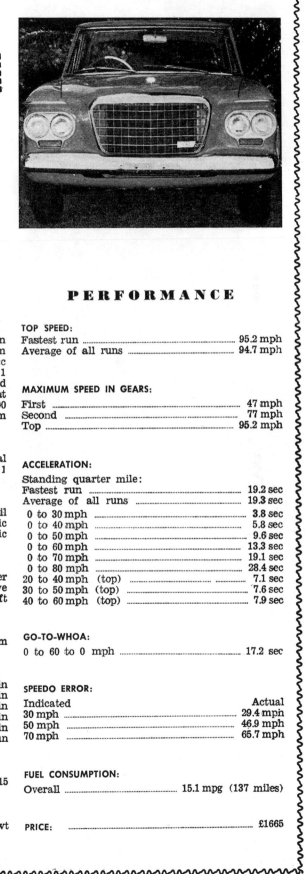

SPECIFICATIONS

ENGINE:
Cylinders .... eight, vee formation
Bore and Stroke .... 90.4 by 82.5 mm
Cubic capacity .... 4247 cc
Compression ratio .... 7.5 to 1
Valves .... pushrod overhead
Carburettor .... two-barrel downdraught
Power at rpm .... 180 at 4500
Maximum torque .... 260 ft/lb at 2800rpm

TRANSMISSION:
Type .... three-speed, manual
Rear axle ratio .... 3.07 to 1

SUSPENSION:
Front .... independent coil
Rear .... semi elliptic
Shocker .... telescopic

STEERING:
Type .... cam and roller
Turns, 1 to 1 .... five
Circle 42ft

BRAKES:
Type .... drum

DIMENSIONS:
Wheelbase 9ft 5in
Track, front 4ft 9in
Track, rear 4ft 8in
Length 15ft 8in
Width 5ft 11½in
Height 4ft 7¾in

TYRES:
Size .... 6.40 by 15

WEIGHT:
Dry .... 26½ cwt

PERFORMANCE

TOP SPEED:
Fastest run .... 95.2 mph
Average of all runs .... 94.7 mph

MAXIMUM SPEED IN GEARS:
First .... 47 mph
Second .... 77 mph
Top .... 95.2 mph

ACCELERATION:
Standing quarter mile:
Fastest run .... 19.2 sec
Average of all runs .... 19.3 sec
0 to 30 mph .... 3.8 sec
0 to 40 mph .... 5.8 sec
0 to 50 mph .... 9.6 sec
0 to 60 mph .... 13.3 sec
0 to 70 mph .... 19.1 sec
0 to 80 mph .... 28.4 sec
20 to 40 mph (top) .... 7.1 sec
30 to 50 mph (top) .... 7.6 sec
40 to 60 mph (top) .... 7.9 sec

GO-TO-WHOA:
0 to 60 to 0 mph .... 17.2 sec

SPEEDO ERROR:

Indicated	Actual
30 mph	29.4 mph
50 mph	46.9 mph
70 mph	65.7 mph

FUEL CONSUMPTION:
Overall .... 15.1 mpg (137 miles)

PRICE: £1665

MS ROAD TEST

STUDEBAKER HAWK

An economy car it ain't.

Although the words "Studebaker" and "Economy" have been synonymous for time beyond the memory of the present generation of auto buyers, the firm has nearly always managed to have a "Class" car in the line ... a car which appeals to a limited market composed of those who want something solid, not too radical and representing the traditional 'custom' craftsmanship of the early automobile industry.

This year, the Gran Turismo Hawk is in the niche filled in the past by such stalwarts as the President Straight Eights.

Its price is well up in the Luxury range; it is available in only one body style; it is unlike anything else in the stable and it is offered with such a wide variety of options that it must be considered the nearest thing to a "custom" the average dealer would care to handle. These characteristics certainly qualify the Hawk as a topflight bird and it must be considered along with the Continental, Thunderbird and suchlike as a special interest automobile.

Unlike the Avanti, which has also been set aside in that

category of personal cars, the Hawk is not going to mark its owner as one by whom the new is first tried. Its basic body shell is by far the oldest still used in the industry, stemming directly from the Raymond Loewy Studebaker creation of 1953. However, such is the validity of intelligent design, ten years later after a few face-lifts and trim alterations, the Hawk is a highly attractive automobile. A squared-off nose and top treatment keep it related to other current shapes and the whole effect is one of conservative modernity. Actually this possibly-contradictory description seems the only fair way to sum up the entire automobile.

Studebaker has made the most of what it had on hand. And what it had on hand it sincerely believed in. "While other companies are retreating from their much advertised advances into new metals, new engine designs and transmission locations, and going back to their precious concepts," said a Studebaker spokesman," Studebaker has gone ahead perfecting the same principles it has found successful through the years."

This policy, which has been dubbed "There's No Substitute For Cast Iron," by some irreverent employees, has resulted in engine, drive train and chassis components which the owner knows he can trust to have all the "teething" problems removed. The Studebaker buyer doesn't have to wait until next year to see if they have the bugs out . . . the bugs were worked out ten years ago. Which doesn't mean that the Hawk is anachronistic. It is a good, possibly outstanding automobile depending on where it is classified, and it has advanced features found in no other car on the market.

The Hawk is a fairly large car although its lines deceive one into thinking it is smaller. Based on a 120 inch w.b. chassis, of separate frame design, the coupe is 204 inches overall in length. It is only one inch higher than the Avanti, however, and weighs a mere 75 pounds more (3,315 lbs. shipping weight), so it fails to get up into that two ton bracket inhabited by most luxury cars. This essential lightness and the optional "super" suspension provide the saving grace and make the Hawk a vehicle which is head and shoulders above those with which it must be compared in appointments and appeal.

The Hawk's road manners are excellent. It is not a sports car, nor is it, save in name, a true GT. But it is a completely normal-handling (as far as the average American driver is concerned) type with far more controllability and far fewer faults than any comparable car MSI has tested. It understeers, to be sure, but it goes where you aim it if you are in possession of this knowledge, and it does not bring on seasickness by wallowing ungracefully while cornering or in high speed highway cruising (which cannot be said, unfortunately, of everything which comes our way to evaluate). Power steering does not reduce the number of turns lock-to-lock (4.6) as in some models, but it is as inoffensive an intrusion into control as we have encountered. The unit is made by Bendix and is excellent, albeit bulky.

This bulk, plus the space occupied by the Paxton supercharger on the R-2 engine, and other accessories provided occasion for the only adverse comment from any staff member. On seeing the hood opened for the first time and finding the engine almost completely obscured by accessories he said "How'd you like to break down somewhere between Las Vegas and Reno?" And it is true that access to the powerplant itself, even unto changing sparkplugs, appears to be as difficult as in any car on the market. In a day when such complexities are becoming standard, this un-conservative arrangement was less good than we expected from Studebaker.

The rest of the automobile drew nothing but praise, particularly the interior. From somewhere Studebaker has come up with the most-nearly-like-leather plastic we have encountered. The seats, paneling and padded dash are covered in this ultra soft, non-shiny material which only needs the smell of neatsfoot oil to complete the illusion. Both the bucket seats and the rear bench, with armrest concealed in the back cushion, are extremely comfortable and supporting. Rear seat leg room is better than average (27 inches from seat to seat) and three average adults can ride comfortably.

The Stude padded dash is outstanding. The edge of the dash which would be struck in event of an accident is covered with a 3 inch roll of foam rubber, not merely a sharp edge wrapped in a quarter inch of material as is generally the case. The balance of the instrument panel shows equal intelligence. It is vertical, recessed and black. Decorative strips are wood-grained and beautiful with the leather-like covering.

A full set of instruments is before the driver: Tachometer, speedo, water temperature, fuel gage, oil pressure, ammeter, clock. No idiot lights.

It is a distinct pleasure to be able to keep tabs on the alternator, engine oil pressure and water temperature while motoring at high speed between Las Vegas and

Reno, as far as the staff of this publication goes. A deep bow also goes to Studebaker for recognizing that reflections in the windshield are not only annoying but dangerous. Flat black and recessed panels are the answer. The toggle switches are neatly identified and uniquely easy to operate.

The simulated wood trim is used on door panels and the whole interior feel is one of high quality.

In performance, the Hawk is not fantastic, but is in keeping with the previously used descriptive, conservatively modern. Depending on the engine, transmission and rear end ratio chosen, it can be either a pretty hot machine away from the spotlight or an easy high speed crûiser.

Studebaker is proud of the fact that it builds custom cars, so you face a tremendous array of possibilities when selecting or ordering. Our test car was a cruiser with 3.31 rear end gears, 4-speed transmission (close ratio) and the R-2 supercharged 304 cubic inch engine but you can go way down in gears to 4.55 or up to 3.07 with 3-or 4-speed manual boxes, and there is a choice of automatics with either column mounted or floor mounted control. The engine choice is between 289 cubic inchers or the 304 cubic inch versions developed for the Avanti, blown or unblown. The two new new ones are designated. R-3 (blown) and R-4 (unblown).

By comparison with the rest of the industry Studebaker's 304 inch engine is small, almost everybody else has at least a hundred cubes over it. The Paxton blower adds considerable thrust through the entire range from off-idle up, but careful gear selection is necessary to get the most out of this combination. The situation is analogous to that found in many sports cars where a small engine of pretty high efficiency has to be worked all the time to equal the loafing output of a really big powerplant.

With the 3.31 gears we were forced to rev the engine up to about 2,000 and slip the clutch a little to get good starts. On the highway, however, cruising at 70 mph, the tach hovered around 3,000 and there was plenty of room on the dial. Top speed runs were not made with the Hawk but it is obviously fast enough to violate the speed limit in any state but Nevada. Acceleration, considering the final drive ratio, is highly adequate.

Braking is most commendable. Compared to other 'personal' cars, it is phenomenal. Dunlop-engineered Bendix discs on the front with conventional drums at the rear, are superb in action and fade quality. Tires leave a little to be desired but the company plainly states in it's owner instruction that the standard equipment tires are for ordinary driving only and that heavy-duty tires are recommended for high speed touring (another honest approach which prejudiced us in favor of the company and its cars). The fact that the Hawk (and all other Studes) use 15 inch wheels (for which a great variety of superior tires are available) is also commendable.

Withal, the concensus of the staff was that the R-2 Hawk is a handsome, refined and extremely roadable car. It may not have the brute strength of some and certainly does not have the obvious flash of others, but, especially with the optional heavy-duty suspension and brakes, it will get you there and back fast as you want to travel in comfort and safety. It is indicative that our biggest complaint was that the turn indicator was not loud enough to be heard, and the tell-tales too dim.

What else do you want, air conditioning?

Well, that's available too, if you'll settle for an unsupercharged engine. Conservatively modern, did we say?

CAR: *STUDEBAKER HAWK 'R2'*
PRICE AS TESTED: *$3976.14*

SPECIFICATIONS

1. GENERAL CONFIGURATION

Body Material: *STEEL*   Engine Location: *FRONT*
Chassis Type: *BOX-SECTION,* Warranty: *24 MO,*
        LADDER   *24,000 MI.*

2. CAPACITIES, WEIGHTS AND DIMENSIONS

Fuel: *18 GAL.*   Test Weight: *3315 (WET)*
Oil: *5 QT.*   Wheelbase: *120.5"*
Water: *17 QT.*   Width: *71"*
Tire Size: *6.70 X 15* Length: *204"*
Turning Radius: *21.3'* Height: *53.8"*

3. ENGINE

Configuration: *V8*   Horsepower: *NOT AVAIL.*
Valves: *OHV*   Torque: *NOT AVAIL.*
Bore & Stroke: *3.56 X 3.62* Comp. Ratio: *9:1*
Displacement: *4770 C.C.* Main Bearings: *5*

4. POWER TRANSMISSION

Gearbox: *4 SPEED*   Axle Type: *LIVE*
Synchro: *ALL*   Final Drive Ratio: *3.31:1*

5. SUSPENSION

Front: *IND. COIL*   Rear: *SOLID AXLE,*
    SPRINGS   *SEMI-ELLIPTIC*
                        SPRINGS

6. BRAKES

Type: *DISC (FRONT)*   Area: *377 SWEPT*
    DRUM (REAR)   *105 SQ."*

7. PERFORMANCE

0-30: *3.1*   Top Speed: *150+ (MFG)*
0-60: *6.7*   Mileage Range: *12/16*
0-90: *13.8*   Standing ¼ Mi.: *14.4*

CONTINUED FROM PAGE 74

can't honestly recommend this for the heavier convertible. The power-to-weight ratio would fall to a lower level than most people are willing to accept.

Studebaker's Flightomatic transmission is a simplified version of the Borg-Warner unit, combining a torque converter and 3-speed gearbox. Although "L" and "D" are the only forward positions marked on the quadrant, considerable manual control is possible. Starting in "L" and shifting to "D" causes the box to go directly from 1st to 3rd. To obtain 2nd on demand, start in "L," then move to "D" and *immediately* pull the lever back into "L." This engages and holds 2nd as long as road speed doesn't drop below 20 mph.

Interior roominess has always been a strong point of the Lark, even in the convertible. The seating is exceptionally comfortable. Because the cushions are well off the floor, the driving position relative to the pedals is less critical than usual. Consequently, the driver has more leeway to place himself the distance he likes from the steering wheel.

The Daytona's special fillip is, of course, its bucket-seated, vinyl-finished passenger compartment. The dash is standard Lark but with a wood-like treatment for the instrument and glove box panels, while the front seats and divider console are borrowed from the Hawk. This blending of parts from two models is a boon for smokers;

there's one ash tray at the center of the dash and another in the console, less than a foot away!

We found the body quite solid for a soft-top model. The panel fit was within reasonable tolerances and we noticed very little structural twist or shake on rough roads. A minor but revealing point about the coachwork was the ease with which the windows operated. Like more present-day convertibles (and so-called hard-tops, for that matter), our Daytona had heavy chromed framing around the glass. Yet the windows could be raised and lowered with no more effort than in most sedans.

The Daytona, like all specialty vehicles from the Monza, Signet and Futura to the 300-H, appeals to the man who would like a sports car but has to be realistic about passenger accommodations. We feel there are better cars in this category for those who appreciate the subtleties of fine handling, i.e., the Hawk.

But the car's faults are no worse than those many people have accepted for years in full-size cars. In fact, its feeling of heaviness might be regarded with favor by drivers who consider weight an advantage.

And, we do have to give the Daytona high marks on roominess and body quality. The convertible provided an acid test on these points and came through superbly. For those who value such things above the ultimate in cornering ability, it's a car worth consideration. ■

CAR LIFE ROAD TEST

PERFORMANCE

Top speed (est), mph	100
2nd (4500)	74
1st (4500)	45

ACCELERATION

0-30 mph, sec	4.1
0-40	6.3
0-50	9.4
0-60	12.9
0-70	17.6
0-80	25.0
Standing ¼ mile	18.9
speed at end	72.5

FUEL CONSUMPTION

Normal range, mpg	17/21

SPEEDOMETER ERROR

30 mph, actual	30.0
60 mph	58.4
90 mph	91.4

CALCULATED DATA

Lb/hp (test wt)	21.3
Cu ft/ton mile	97.4
Mph/1000 rpm	24.1
Engine revs/mile	2490
Piston travel, ft/mile	1350
Car Life wear index	33.6

PULLING POWER

4th, lb/ton @ mph	235 @ 64
3rd	355 @ 49
2nd	575 @ 30
Total drag at 60 mph, lb	158

STUDEBAKER DAYTONA

SPECIFICATIONS

List price	$2814
Price, as tested	3149
Curb weight, lb	3530
Test weight	3835
distribution, %	58.8/41.2
Tire size	6.70-15
Tire capacity, lb	4460
Brake swept area	282
Engine type	V-8, ohv
Bore & stroke	3.56 x 3.25
Displacement, cu in	259.2
Compression ratio	8.5
Bhp @ rpm	180 @ 4500
equivalent mph	108.4
Torque, lb-ft	260 @ 2800
equivalent mph	67.5

DIMENSIONS

Wheelbase, in	109
Tread, f and r	57.4/56.6
Over-all length, in	184
width	71.2
height	58.1
equivalent vol, cu ft	440
Frontal area, sq ft	23.0
Ground clearance, in	7.0
Steering ratio, o/a	22.5
turns, lock to lock	4.4
turning circle, ft	37
Hip room, front	2 x 23.0
Hip room, rear	41.5
Pedal to seat back, max	40.0
Floor to ground	13.0
Luggage vol, cu ft	14.2
Fuel tank capacity, gal	18.0

EXTRA-COST OPTIONS

Automatic transmission, radio, wsw tires, crankcase ventilation.

GEAR RATIOS

3rd (1.00), overall	3.31
2nd (1.47)	4.86
1st (2.40)	7.95
1st (2.40 x 2.15)	17.1

ACCELERATION & COASTING

[Graph: MPH vs ELAPSED TIME IN SECONDS showing 1st, 2nd, 3rd gear acceleration curves and coasting, with SS¼ marked. Vertical axis MPH from 10 to 90, horizontal axis elapsed time in seconds from 5 to 45.]